Karmic Dates and

Momentary Mates:

The Astrology of the Fifth House

By Jessica Shepherd

Third Edition, 2015
Published by
Moonkissd Astrology
www.moonkissd.com

Cover: *Paolo and Francesca* by Giuseppe Poli,
Accademia Carrara, Comune di Bergamo, Photographed
by Kiorau.
Design: Nada Orlic

To my husband, John, for his dream about karmic
connections that inspired this book, his encouragement,
and his loving support.

Preface

What if we could see the invisible cords that tied us together?

Speaking to me from that half-awake, moonlit space, my husband recounted a dream.

"There was a woman in it, an Oracle, who possessed a special gift: she could see the connections that tied people together. These cords of light floated between two people and they varied in size, texture, and color, depending on the essence and strength of the bond. Some connections were dense and others light. Some people had many cords tying them to others, while others had only a few. The Oracle could do more than see these invisible connections, though. She could cut the bonds tying two people together. And people would travel the world over for her ability to sever connections, which once broken, gave them peace and freedom." John paused. "I think this dream message is meant for you, to write about in your next book."

I had just published *A Love Alchemist's Notebook*, a book about how I attracted my soul mate, in which I introduced the idea of karmic mates—partners not meant to be in our life forever, but with whom we share an ancient contract to exchange a gift, lesson, awakening, or teaching for a time. But recently I had begun exploring shared short-term karma through the astrological fifth house, and the connections I was making were exciting. I discovered I could glimpse the mysterious x-factor behind those relationships that, like a comet or supernova, burned hot and bright and then died young. I could also describe the elusive something that keeps us hanging on too long, long after love has turned to attachment, and explain the necessity of endings. *Not all relationships are meant to be lifelong.* I could identify whether someone had a higher than average amount of business to finish with others, and therefore needed to be open to having a number of different relationships. For those who felt socially pressured to be monogamous, this information was wildly validating, even liberating.

The subject of karmic cords had struck a chord with me and with clients, who came to me for consultations and asked, "Is my current partner my soul mate or karmic mate?" Through the astrological fifth house, the invisible bonds that tie us to others are made visible. I had more to say about the subject, as John's dream foretold.

That is the origin of this book. We've all known "the one who got away." We've each wondered why a relationship couldn't continue, why a person entered our life when we were unavailable or the relationship seemed impossible, or why a "meant to be" relationship simply wasn't. More than love affairs and their demise, this book is also about the revitalizing power of joy, creativity, passion, romance, and the people who stimulate that in us—even for just a time. Imagine: Some connections in your life exist for the pure joy of helping you to grow and reach your potential through pleasure, creativity, and love!

Our most spectacular heartbreaks can deliver great spiritual leaps. Culturally, we tend to favor beginnings while sweeping death and endings under the rug. We also tend to favor monogamy and long-term partnerships, often labeling our short-term relationships as failures, negating another's impact on our life and denying ourselves the opportunity for deeper understanding. Instead of allowing our ex-partners to remain a bitter footnote in our histories, we might try to poke around with fresh eyes and bring light to soulful lessons learned. I've included a brief section at the end with a few ideas about this. People deliver marvelous gifts into our lives— even those who leave. Isn't it a wonderful thing?

Throughout this text, you'll notice I use the word karma liberally. You don't have to believe in reincarnation to appreciate the idea that you may have invisible connections with others that defy your understanding. Pondering if you could have a contract with another that extends beyond this lifetime could give you pause, and with this question I'm hoping to stir not only your love for mystery, but also your awe and wonder. Why? Awe and wonder always inspire greater insight into the heart.

Finally, there is one practical note to address before you proceed. Astrology is a vast subject. My goal was to make this information accessible to laypeople and students of astrology alike. You won't need a degree in astrological studies to understand this book, but to get the most from it you will need your birth chart. For instructions on how to obtain a free copy of your birth chart and locate your fifth house planet(s) and sign, please refer to the Appendix at the end of this book.

Section 1

The Compelling Attraction of Karma

My client arrived for a 1 p.m. appointment and rang the doorbell of my Viennese flat. Unfamiliar with how the European entryway worked, I held the buzzer down for a few seconds, and just to make sure she'd gotten in I stepped into the foyer of the apartment building. That's when it hit me—a scent so strong it could've knocked me out. My nose told me it was a strong mix of patchouli and lavender; my sixth sense told me it was mildly unnerving—a scent not entirely unpleasant, but not entirely pleasant, either.

I welcomed Tara and her mysteriously strong perfume. Taking her coat and moving into the kitchen to brew some relaxing lemon balm tea and extend an invitation of dark chocolate, I asked, "What is that scent you're wearing?" Tara replied, "It's called Karma, a perfume I wear." Not skipping a beat, I exclaimed, "You have some strong karma!" She sheepishly grinned.

What is karma? The simple answer is: cause and effect. Spiritual teachers say our actions from far beyond this time and space send a ripple into the future. Unless you're talking about the "instant karma" of, say, giving someone a few bucks on the street and then getting a promotion later that day, karma is linked with reincarnation, the idea that we have past and possibly future lives.

Since karma substantiates cause for having past and future lives, we can surmise that there's no way we can complete all our karma in one lifetime. Our karma continues to unfold through cause and effect in the events and relationships of our present lives. Many believe nothing in this universe is without karma. Every action creates a reaction. Even a non-action can create karma. Think about an alcoholic mother passed out on the sofa who forgets to pick up her child from school, or the big opportunity you let slip through your fingers out of fear. Failure to act creates karma, too. Since we are incarnating on planet Earth at this time, we all have karma. It's nothing to feel guilty about. Even if we decided to shut ourselves off from the world and become monks, we could not avoid participating in cause and effect. The desire to cloister ourselves away from life would require a balancing effect in the future. There is simply no escaping this cycle.

What does karma have to do with my relationships, you ask? Think of one major event in your life that didn't involve an important relationship. Impossible, right? Most of our significant karma involves other people. We share karma with other people, and sometimes many other people. Karma is the hidden thread running through our relationships, tying us together in mysterious ways. What else could explain the experiences of instant attraction, split-second gut feelings of familiarity, comfort, love, or even animosity?

The cosmic sticky glue of karma compels attractions (and aversions) that bring us back together to finish business, exchange soul gifts, and complete soul lessons. It compels that wonderful feeling of deep like and true love. It also compels revenge, jealousy, rivalry, annoyance, and negativity. From the perspective of reincarnation, if we didn't have enough sticky glue to compel a future meeting, we wouldn't bother to fall in love, make babies, or take a risk on a total stranger. The attraction of karma compels phone numbers and email addresses to be exchanged, first, second and third dates to be made, nights to be spent together, and babies to be born. We need a strong attraction to do this kind of deep soul work together. One perfumed whiff of shared karma compels that some kind of contract be established, once again.

So if you're wondering how you'll know when you're under the compelling attraction of karma, it begins with an instant attraction, affinity, or aversion. It begins with that pheremonally fabulous lingering scent that you just can't get out of your nose. Like a perfume invisibly wafting up a staircase, this person's chemistry may bowl you over with the power of its allure. It may be erotically exciting for you. It may be unnerving. It may be mysterious. Above all, it may be something stronger, and more meaningful, than you suspect.

Karmic Mates and the Fifth House

Everything's a gamble, love most of all. —Tess Gerritsen

Nothing takes the taste out of peanut butter like unrequited love. —Charlie Brown

Like some wines, our love could neither mature nor travel. —Graham Greene

Some of us think holding on makes us strong, but sometimes it is letting go. —Herman Hesse

The fifth house of: Self-expression, creativity, performance, risk, speculation and gambling, short-term love affairs, dating and courtship, romantic passion, children, spontaneity, pleasures, recreation, theater, entertainment, drama, karma surrounding right use of will.

Corresponding to the sign: Leo.

Archetypes of Leo: The Lover, Performer, Child, Clown, Primadonna, Spoiled Brat.

Ruled by: The Sun, center of the solar system.

Characterized by the urge to: Experience joy, romance, fun, the renewing power of pleasure. Be seen and creatively express oneself. See oneself through another's eyes. Experience vitality through the creative process. Live uninhibitedly, spontaneously, and open-heartedly. Live in the present moment.

When not navigated with awareness we: Become addicted to novelty, spontaneity, and change; fear boredom, have a need for continuous short-term relationship thrills, diversions, distractions. At worst, true intimacy skills are stunted by a continual merry-go-round of lovers.

By the time we leave our teenage years and loves behind, most of us realize that not all relationships are meant to last. Not to say that these people weren't significant. Think about your first love and the great gift they gave you: love. They gave you their adoration, fascination, and affection... until they gave those same things to your best friend. By the time we're in our late twenties or early thirties, we've each encountered "the one that got away." These people who we thought were meant to be, and now seem destined to remain a kind, or unfortunately bitter, footnote in the story our life.

Welcome to the fifth house of romance and short-term love affairs! The falling-in-love house, where exchanging our life stories with a stranger can lead to mad passionate sex and even true love. Initially, a fifth house romance is a wild ride—there's nothing they do that doesn't make our heart do backflips. Their taste in music, the way they order their steak, and all those crazy interests that they have somehow seem less crazy and, well, more intriguing. When they share their demons with us, we think, "Ahhh, finally a person with depth [never mind the skull and crossbones hanging above their bed]." Wowed by the impact of their energy on ours, when they tell us they're forty and still live at home, we're still thinking, "How sweet."

Most of my understanding of the fifth house I owe to my teacher, Steven Forrest, who gave me the framework for exploring this idea astrologically. Isabel Hickey also influenced me, when in her monumental book *Astrology, A Cosmic Science*, she said something very interesting about the fifth house: "This is a house of hidden karma;

hidden karma specifically involving how we've misused our will and the love principle."

When I came across Hickey's definition, I was intrigued by the "hidden" part. Leo, the natural ruler of this house, is an expressive, openhearted, and loving sign (everyone knows that Leos are terrible at keeping secrets). Then I understood: The karma was hidden behind the dramatic excitement and mutual enthrallment of falling for another person. The sexual chemistry, the instant attraction... like a film noir, I imagined a person with Venus in the fifth house reporting a crime of the heart: *Officer, I was having such a good time and she was so damn good-looking, I just didn't see it coming. She charmed me with her magnetic personality and made me feel like a million bucks, then stole my cash and left me with heart in hand.*

There's no astrological translation needed for this heist of the heart; this is what happens in reality. The one-night stand, the fling, the failed romance, the unrequited love affair... all are common expressions of the fifth house. But as Hickey points out, if we have planets here we must take extra care not to misuse our will when it comes to love—which is exactly what often happens when we are young and inexperienced. In fact, troubling fifth house planets approach love a lot like teenagers. Enthusiastic about love and naïve in approach, notorious for their lack of discernment and ruled by hormones, fifth house planets can get into hot water faster than you can say Britney Spears (whose Aquarius Moon is in the fifth house). Out of wedlock children are one such consequence of unruly fifth house planets.

Whereas seventh house planets revolve around questions of trust, such as can I trust you as a life mate, fifth house planets revolve around questions of shared affection, joy, and spontaneity, like: Do I have fun and enjoy myself with you? While "who would be a really great date to the new *Star Wars* movie?" isn't a qualifying question for a life mate, it is the first step in surrendering to the joy, romance, and enlivening energy of being with another person. To begin a relationship, we need to have a good time together and enjoy shared company. But if we choose to initiate a committed relationship solely on the basis of shared sexual chemistry and the fact that we both like Stephen King novels, we're in serious trouble.

People with fifth house planets have a learning curve in the who-to-date department. The dating process is a learning curve about who and how to date, and as the saying goes, you can't make an omelet without breaking a few eggs. Ideally we open up, share our authentic selves, and come from the heart. We surrender to the joy of letting another person in, all the while knowing it's a risk. We may have our hearts broken. We may find our true love. Let's not forget, this is the house of speculation, risk, and gambling. Fifth house hearts ride the rollercoaster of love. Hopefully we enjoy the ride, and we get off a little dizzy, high, and a bit wiser than when we got on.

Having fifth house planets doesn't doom anyone to a lifetime of dating and short-term love affairs, but it does suggest the necessity of friendships, lovers, playmates, and creative partnerships—for a time. These partnerships may last a month or a decade (time is elastic in the fifth house, and short-term could mean anything less than forever), but they are no less significant for your interpersonal and spiritual development than a partner in marriage. Nowadays, a marriage partner could be a short-term partner, too.

Then there's the question of hidden karma. Maybe you can easily entertain the idea that all of your significant relationships are not "new news," that there are people with whom we have made prior life contracts to meet. Of course, we may never be able to prove this factually, but the critical mass of people with regression experiences makes a very strong case for past lives.

Karma is certainly a mysterious force that complicates, informs, and weaves itself, snakelike, through this lifetime (and perhaps the next) for as long as we're alive and making choices. Some of us have more short-term shared relationship karma than others, and having fifth house planets—with their hunger for heart-opening connections—alerts us to this possibility.

Having a planet in the fifth house alerts us to potential immaturity in love matters, but it's no judgment on our spiritual maturity. His Holiness the Dalai Lama has fifth house karma. Unsurprisingly, it's Jupiterian: His short-term shared karma revolves around the auspices of blessings, divine protection, faith, spirituality, and luck, as is appropriate for the planet of Kings, Royalty, Priests, and Gurus. He shares karma with people of influence and affluence, and His Holiness has karmic mates in high places. While Jupiter's luck has been clear for him, it hasn't been a bed of roses, either. Leaders have welcomed him and granted him asylum in their countries, and celebrities have taken him under their wings, but the Dalai Lama fled his own country—his hand forced by the actions of less benefic Jupiter figures.

We are not the Dalai Lama, with his problems and his spiritual path; we can only speculate as to why he has this karma. We won't know why we share the karma we do with others, but using astrology, we can identify the nature of our shared relationship karma by looking at the planets in our fifth house—as well as the pitfalls, shadows, and things to watch out for with that planet. As with the Dalai Lama, we can paint a fairly clear picture of the type of character we share short-term karma with— should we share it. Having planets in the fifth house alerts us to the fact that we may have unfinished business with one or several people who share the nature and behaviors of that planet-sign combination. What if we don't have a planet here? We can look to the sign on our fifth house cusp, as well as the ruling planet of that sign (to identify these, see Appendix at the end of this book), which also alerts us to the quality of karma we share.

Karma is nothing to feel guilty about. We all have it. After all, if the Dalai Lama has unfinished business, it's probably not such a bad thing that you have it, too. Sharing karma is both a gift and an obligation. The gift is an ability to receive and exchange a teaching, blessing, or learning. The obligation is to learn to recognize when such a relationship has outlived its usefulness, and to let it go with respect to all involved. Just because a relationship is short-term, doesn't make it any less valuable, precious, or worthy of an honorable ending.

Karmic Mates, Why We Have Them, and What to Do About It

Do any action totally and you are free of it. You don't look back because there is nothing to see... Be total and you will be free. —Osho

When we are substantially attracted to someone enough to enter into a relationship, we undoubtedly share a level of karma. Clearly, we must share karma with all our important relationships. We share karma with people who, over the course of a lifetime, help us to self-actualize and reach our dreams with love and support. I call these people our soul mates—people who hold us in love for as long as time allows. Karmic mates are "time-of-life partners"; these partnerships are eventually meant to end. Karmic mates may be a form of soul mates, for we certainly share soul contracts with them—but while there is no ending to the love story with soul mates (save death), karmic partners have an expiration date.

Some cultures make the distinction between those "forever" partners we commit to and time-of-life partners (maybe our culture should—it might take away some of our romantic confusion!). In Germany, where there is little to no social pressure to marry, those companions partnered with us for a time are called *lebensabschnittsgefaehrte*. That long word translates as "time-of-life partner" and Germans openly distinguish their time-of-life partners from lifelong ones. My Austrian friend, Sven, is married to a German woman; he explained that when a person is asked about their relationship status, and they reply that they are with a time-of-life partner, they literally are saying, "I am not available today... but I may be tomorrow." Ah: momentary mates.

A relationship that lasts for a period of time can be just as exciting or fulfilling as a "forever" partner. Our momentary mate may be a romantic interest, a weekend fling, a short-term love affair, or a person with whom we schlep to Ikea and set up house for a time. Karmic mates wear other guises, too, besides sexual partners. You can recognize them by the joy, buzz, attraction, and excitement they stimulate in you—the initial, heady yeast of relationships. They may be a playmate or a muse, inspiring shared artistry and creativity. They may be someone who shares a hobby or interest that our primary partner doesn't, but through sharing, we grow stronger and shine brighter. We can share karma with our elementary school teacher, our best friend, our therapist, and maybe even our pet! Through their belief in us, confidence in our talents and abilities, or any positive heart-centered emotion, we just feel good being around them.

The karmic mate is always a catalyst for our growth. By virtue of the conversations and experiences we share over a brief period of time, we end up making a change in our lives. Playmate, muse, catalyst, boss, lover, roommate, friend... while they don't stick around forever, their impact on our lives can be profound.

Can you think of anyone who made a profound impact on your life, but who you now see infrequently, or you may never see again? Even the seemingly insignificant players on the stage of your life, the "extras" in your life story, can be karmic mates. I once had a college roommate, a bossy loud-mouthed Italian. We had little in common, but she was a lot of fun. She was a recreation major, a specialist at play and partying, but she was there for me during a very emotionally difficult time. My mother was dying of cancer and I was falling apart, using a combination of art therapy and anti-depressants to help myself through it. One extremely hard day she said to me, "Even when things are terribly difficult and threaten to shut you down, you try new things. That's why I'm not worried about you. You'll get through this." There are people in life with whom a momentary conversation mobilizes a year of hope, and this was one. She encouraged me, though I'm certain she has no idea about the impact of her faith in me. We weren't casual friends or even best friends (best friends belong to the astrological seventh house), though not for trying. We tried to turn our relationship into something it wasn't, eventually causing petty arguments and forcing a split.

Many of us try to turn our momentary mates into lifelong partners, with questionable results. A friend of mine, Emma, is married to a man with Taurus Moon in the fifth house (opposed by Venus in Scorpio). Before Emma and

Dave met, Dave had a large number of short-term women partners with whom he is still friends to this day (echoes of eleventh house Venus in Scorpio), and though they didn't marry, he co-parented a child with one of these women. Many of these relationships lasted too long, with love and affection transforming into compulsive battling. He said of one particularly painful relationship, "That relationship was supposed to last three months, and it ended up lasting five years." Instead of being happily stuck together, they unhappily stuck together.

Unfortunately, staying in a partnership that has outlived its purpose has the effect of making us dumber, not wiser. Even the choices we think are right come out wrong. Two people stay together "for the kids," only to discover years later that the kids wished we'd have found the courage to divorce, to seek out true happiness and fulfillment in our own lives. Yet, nature has a way of helping us release these mates. After the karma is exchanged, we often simply *fall out of love*. This is the usual way of things. As the relationship becomes untenable, the little things that we once loved about the other now repel us, and the compelling attraction dissipates. We cannot find the love in our heart to justify all the dissatisfaction and antagonism we feel. We realize that the person we love, no matter how wonderful and desirable he or she is or was, is not the partner we want to be with for the rest of our lives.

Like Dave and his karmic mate, we can spend years trying to get what we need but the other cannot give—*because the relationship had outlived its purpose.* Unlike soul mate relationships—those relationships where a partner lovingly holds a mirror up to us, holding us accountable to the highest version of ourselves—we can spend years trying to fix our karmic relationship, and become the most unflattering version of ourselves.

My teacher Steven Forrest once shared this parable: A *Rinpoche* (a Buddhist teacher) was visiting a Zen retreat center to give a dharma talk, and he took his place as the teacher on a small area rug at the front of a classroom full of students. When the session broke, the *Rinpoche* got up to get a drink of water and chatted with other students. The meditation gong sounded to return to the seat, but when he did, the *Rinpoche* was surprised to discover someone had taken his sitting rug. His first response was indignation: "How dare someone take *my* rug!" Fortunately (he is a *Rinpoche*, after all), he realized how silly he was being. It was not his rug—but because he was sitting on it, because it was with him for a period of time that morning, he became attached to it. We grow attached to our mates, and to our thoughts and feelings about them. But like the *Rinpoche*'s area rug, our mates are not ours any more than we are theirs, and when love and affection become compulsion and willfulness, there's a risk of creating *future* shared karma.

Anytime we substitute our heart and freely given love with willfulness, love goes awry. So how do we work on resolving our stubborn attachments to karmic mates? First, we must understand that when a relationship causes us more pain than joy, holding onto it will create future pain and suffering. The other part is deceptively simple: Be present to your heart's full truth. Don't hold on, look back, or project into the future. Be complete in yourself in this moment; be complete in your feelings and choices right now. Become one with the present moment—mentally, spiritually, and emotionally. Make decisions from that place, and you will enter karma-free zone. Even though it may hurt your heart to make a hard and truthful call to end a pairing, truth is a freedom, gifting you with more openness, joy, and availability to life.

Am I in a Karmic Partnership?

All relationships have some element of karma, so how do we know if we're in a relationship with an expiration date? Initially, it can be hard to tell. Here's a common sense checklist (adapted from my book, *A Love Alchemist's Notebook: Magical Secrets for Drawing Your True Love Into Your Life*) for identifying whether you are in a karmic partnership (you will also want to read the section, "Planets and Signs in the Fifth House").

-You experience a compulsive mood or emotion unique to only this relationship, which you don't normally experience. Around this person, you may feel caretaking, insecure, chatty, irrational, moody, exceptionally beautiful, larger or smaller-than-life. When apart, you are free of this condition.

-You are attached to trying to get something (attention, affection, love, commitment) from them. When you don't get it, you feel nutty.

-Your partnership elicits irrational behavior in one or both of you. You feel powerless to stop it.

-You know this relationship won't last, yet you cannot seem to tear yourself away.

-Friends and loved ones say they no longer recognize you, or that you've changed (not for the better) since you've been with this person.

-You experience compelling magnetism, and even love. But while you are attracted to certain parts of them, you do not fully accept them.

A Relationship Without a Future

"Karma is habit," I wrote at the top of the intake form while preparing for a new client. It was an intuitive inkling, and I've learned to listen to those.

Nita, an attractive sixty-four-year-old woman, arrived in my home office wearing a red dress with perfectly manicured nails, great makeup, and a blonde mane of hair. She'd booked an appointment after reading about karmic relationships in *A Love Alchemist's Notebook*, and she was certain she was in one. She and her current partner had been married for twenty years when he left her for another woman. Despite the pain of the betrayal she and their children experienced, in the years since he left she hadn't been able to fully move on. He called her often, expressing how much he missed her and the kids, and yet he wouldn't put both feet back into the boat again. She told me that he was unable to be the person she wanted him to be. "Two days ago," she said, "I put my foot down and decided to break up with him again."

Nita had a fifth house South Node in the sign of Gemini. The South Node and its sign describe a set of easy, habitual behaviors that we can unconsciously fall into. Someone with the South Node in the fifth house may over-focus on love affairs, easily getting caught up in the pleasures and romantic melodrama of the moment. A Gemini South Node person dissipates their energy by running around in circles in both life and love.

Nita validated all of this, admitting that she had a strong habit of mentally mulling things over and over. A South Node placement here also suggests she has fifth house shared karma, and of a certain quality: She might enjoy a connection with a young person, a twin soul, or someone who felt like a sibling (Gemini) who was clever, possibly immature, and preferred spontaneity over-committing to the future. As I mentioned the "lover as sibling" piece, her eyes became round and watery—this man had always felt like a brother to her. Nita also had a tendency to live in the moment instead of making long-term plans. As a result of her relationship focus, she found keeping her long-term goals on track difficult (North Node Sagittarius, eleventh house), such as the Master's degree in Psychology that she'd been attempting to complete for years.

The South Node holds the repository of our soul's heart memory, which extends beyond this lifetime, starting up like an old phonograph record waiting for resolution again. I imagined two kids in love with stars in their eyes, dreaming of a future, but never having that future get off the ground. That described this life, too! I juxtaposed two sixteen-year-old kids dreaming of building a life together against the wisdom of two people reaching midlife who had fulfilled lifelong dreams and goals together, and were happily heading into their golden years. Nita craved a relationship with her wisdom self. As we continued to talk, and I mentioned the idea of fifth house karma involving the misuse of will in love, Nita moved closer to the truth of her karmic "habit." She said, "I am a very willful person. For many years I have been trying to change this man, creating conditions around my love for him. I have not been satisfied, yet I haven't let go. I surrender control in so many other areas of my life, but not in this one."

Nita had previously told me she thought they shared past lives together. Maybe they had. We don't have to know *why* something is the way it is to move beyond a pattern. Many people get hung up on past life connections, justifying their inability leave a difficult or painful relationship because of some mysterious past-life grip it has on them. *Karma is habit.* This is a powerful point to understand about karma. It is not mysterious and out there—it's in the here-and-now. Even with the most difficult relationship, we can resolve and change our future karma by being present right now, and by changing our habitual attitude. Our present-day responses, choices, emotions, and attitudes towards people in our lives and life events always either resolve or create karma.

This brought us to what I had written at the top of her chart, which I now showed her. Nita's actions were compulsive. She was trying to make this relationship work, not out of love, but out of sheer will. Instead of doing the karmic reshuffle with this man, she could follow through on her vision for her life and create a future she loved. Only she could break the habit.

Karma is Habit

The concept of karma can seem so esoteric and out there that it's hard to grasp the everyday reality of it. In ancient Buddhist texts, karma is written as *karma-vipaka*, meaning "action and result." Imagine you have a repetitive fight with your partner. *He never listens*, you think, and you get bent out of shape. We experience karma through our habits, attitudes, and habitual responses. "They aren't listening again" is causing you to shut down and get angry, to lose your cool. *But*, you justify, *they aren't listening!* They may not be. You can choose to work on communication skills. You can take a new action. It's your life, your choice. Our habituated emotional attitudes and responses generate karma. Call it karma, or habit; it's the same thing. If we don't like the results we see in our lives, we need to change the habitual action and choose anew. No karma is so difficult that it can't be resolved by our awareness, presence, and choice in the now.

Section 2

Love-Bombed in the Fifth House

An astrologer friend wrote me the following message: "Help, I've fallen into my fifth house and I can't get up! It feels too good to leave!"

Of course it does! I believe the fifth house experience is connected to our second chakra, the pleasure chakra of sexuality and creativity. When we encounter a fifth house mate's sexy chemistry, we're bowled over and wowed. The problem is, while long-term relationships are meant to wow our whole being—all chakras—our karmic partners hang out mostly in the ooey-gooey feel-good chemistry of our second chakra. A committed relationship cannot vibrate on second chakra bandwidth exclusively; our body cannot take it, and these relationships eventually burn out like a comet.

In her book *Beyond Soul Mates*, author and energy worker Cyndi Dale compares these relationships to comets for their initially fiery and all-encompassing, and then self-combusting nature. Like a comet, your mate comes streaking down from the heavens to meet you, and the partnership feels so amazing and right—until you feel the burn. These relationships are so exclusively tied to the first chakra of sexuality, physical survival, safety, and materiality, Cyndi says, that their myopic focus exhausts us.

So what's the purpose of being love-bombed? These people revitalize us, delivering a super charge of revivifying energy. Just as these chakra centers are the seeds of our primal life force energies, the fifth house is the seat of our willpower, vitality, leadership, and creativity. When a love bomb detonates in your fifth house, you are also being fueled and juiced by a massive upsurge of creative energies, energies that you need in your life to create and step into your full power.

The fifth house is naturally ruled by the Sun—that planetary body holding our creative center, our vital life force, and our volition to live a life by our own design. Have you ever been blown open and revivified by a heart-wrenching love affair that didn't last? Were you surprised to discover that, even if you also experienced heartbreak, the world had become a more alive, lustrous, magnificent version of its former self? This energy is not dependent on your lover, even though he or she was the initial catalyst to get some necessary juice moving again in your life. Maybe you needed to take a new step and lacked the energy. This energy to create, manifest, attract, and move through the world in a more empowered way may have been stimulated by your lover or short-term partner, but it is always present, and yours to use as you choose.

Yes, the karmic mate may blow you open and burn you out, but deeper than the sound and noise, the dramatic highs and lows, he or she has a far more noble purpose: To reignite the spark waiting to be lit inside you.

Creative Catalysts and Other Near Disasters

In chemistry, a chemical catalyst is something that speeds things up without itself getting used up in the process. People can act as catalysts in our lives when they initiate a growth process for us, but remain untouched themselves. Just as the muse stimulates a body of work for the artist, and remains untouched by the creative process him or herself; or the lover calls us with his or her siren song then sails away, leaving us heart-wrecked. Our catalyst doesn't have to do anything but show up.

When others act as a catalyst, they stimulate a growth process in us. They may not ever know the depths of how they've changed our lives, minds, choices, or ways of being. The connection runs deep for us (and maybe just for us), while they may appear to remain superficially untouched. Unrequited love is one example of this. A person who we romantically long for (unbeknownst to the object of affection), but who never becomes a lover, can stimulate new interests, awareness, and directions—even if the relationship seems to be a figment of our imagination, a fluff of fantasy. It doesn't have to be romantic, though often there's an amount of erotic admiration and affection involved. Evening coffees with our beautiful and intelligent art professor might stimulate our desire to pursue a direction in our art, without the professor ever having known his or her impact. Catalysts arrive in many interesting forms, and sometimes unexpectedly.

Their appearance can be a big surprise—as it was for me, when a man who was growing in spiritual guru status reached out to me, declaring his romantic affections. Ian and I had met only once in person, yet he was convinced that he was my soul mate. "I already have a soul mate," I said, which I did. But I was also flattered and intrigued. Every time I thought about this surprising occurrence, I felt a shock of excitement at being admired, and my spiritual curiosity stirred. Why did this stranger—one who was respected in the spiritual community—think he was my soul mate? It's not as if he was wearing a tinfoil hat. He had a sort of metaphysical credibility.

The timing of this contact was interesting on multiple levels. I'd been in a dark time of creative block. I felt stuck, bored. For the first time in years, I had no creative projects inspiring me. Ian's attentions viscerally woke me up. Through intuitive and clairvoyant work, I explored the nature of our relationship without pursuing it in real life. As a result of this imagined connection, I began exploring the topic of past-life karma in relationships, and inspired by the seeds of thought that I had begun while writing *A Love Alchemist's Notebook*—thoughts about learning to identify our karmic relationships—I began writing this book. This man, who I met once and never expect to see again, was a catalyst for my creativity.

This episode proved to be catalytic in more ways than one. I hadn't told my husband about him, and one day Ian instant messaged me while my husband was on my computer. Naturally, John felt hurt and betrayed: Why hadn't I entrusted him with this information? This caused us to examine our trust levels and agreements, our feelings about opposite-sex friendships, our right to privacy and secrets, and our shadows and wounds of trust. It was a painful period of growth for our partnership, but as we held the mirror up for one another, we became more intimate with our shadow selves, and each other.

The time was right, astrologically, in the moving sky: The planet ruling my fifth house (house of karmic mates, creativity) had joined the planet ruling my seventh house

(house of committed partnerships), even as it was utterly unwieldy for my marriage. The karmic mate's arrival isn't always convenient. One day, they pop up on Facebook or in our book group with the potential to rock our world. But no matter how awkward, there is a "right timing" here, for when they show up, we can safely assume that we needed a wake-up call. The Great Creator wants to give us a jolt. We can make the choice to handle with care and, if we are in a relationship, do so without damaging the trust we've established with our partner.

The role of a catalyst is to wake us up, to activate a process inside. As a result of our meeting, we are changed. Through our fifth house mates, we learn the varied, sometimes unexpected and surprising power of self-renewal, awakening us to ourselves and to the spontaneous sacred play of life. But when it comes to "past-life reunions," fair is forewarned. Using past lives to justify a connection can distract us from the present, and even prove damaging to our relationships. In a study, psychologists discovered that when negative events happened to people in relationships who held "destiny beliefs" (say, that destiny brought you together and will keep you together, or they shared a past life and so are meant to be together, today), they were far more disengaged and even withheld ways to support the relationship. Likewise, the study also said when their relationship hit rocky waters, couples who shared *growth beliefs*—the practical idea that relationships grow by working through tough times together—fared far better.

Fortunately, my husband and I worked through this karmic hiccup, but my spiritual curiosity taught me a huge lesson. In Buddhism, there's a word called *Lila* (the play of God). *Lila* sees the world as divine play, and when we get so caught up in watching the three-dimensional show, *Lila* (or illusion), warns us of the danger of confusing the players, the theatrics, the great lighting and alluring staging, the song and dance, with reality itself. Chemistry can be so strong, exciting, and heady that it can take us out of the present moment, potentially causing us to make poor decisions. When that happens, we can step out of the scene by remembering *Lila*— remembering that all is not what it appears to be.

I Can't Get to the Altar: A Fifth House Lament

Carissima has been engaged five times, but each time "had enough good sense to realize that my doubts about each of my fiancés were enough to break off the engagements well before I made it to the altar." She loves romance and dating, and she knows that once married she'll have to leave the glamorous life of the bachelorette behind. So she never does.

Carissima, an aging Italian movie star, is a fictional character in a novel of the same name, but it's easy to recognize the archetype. We enjoy wooing and being wooed, telling our story to someone new… and when we attempt to sustain a relationship, we grow bored after only a brief time, or become scared of losing our freedom, or start cataloguing all the faults and flaws we see in them. We may think, *it's not the right person.* Maybe that's true. Or maybe we're caught up in the thrill-seeking madness of the fifth house.

When I think of this particular fifth house shadow, I recall the cute movie *Fifty First Dates*. In the movie, Drew Barrymore's character wakes up every single day without a memory of the day before. When her love interest, played by Adam Sandler, introduces himself to her, she's as charmed by his story as if she was hearing it for the very first time. Except it's not the first time. She is an amnesiac, and for her every day is their first day together. Sandler's love-struck character soon devises a way to record and playback every day they share, but eventually he realizes that they will never progress. They are permanently stuck at the falling-in-love phase of romantic attraction, and their love will never deepen or go any further.

There are thrills and spine-tingling chills that accompany a new relationship, with all its firsts—its first kisses, first discoveries, and first stories—but as the Sandler character eventually experiences, falling in love with someone who can't envisage any relationship beyond fifty first dates is an exercise in frustration. This makes sense to most of us. We enter the fifth house knowing it leads somewhere, to something *more*. We know we're not supposed to stop here; there's deeper satisfaction to be had in commitment and intimacy (the seventh and eighth houses). But the shadowy fifth house specializes in playing the field, footloose and fancy-free. As opposed to that healthy precursor to intimacy, courtship, when we necessarily keep our options open while we size up potential mates, for the shadowy fifth house the spontaneous thrill of getting to know another is fun—but no one is ever perfect enough to take that leap for (they laugh too loud, talk too much), nor will they ever be. In the shadowy fifth, we suspect someone better is always around the corner, so leave our options permanently open.

Evan, a client with Venus in Taurus in the fifth house (square Jupiter in Leo), was a world traveler with cosmopolitan flair and had that special something that drove women wild. But he wasn't happy. He said he wanted a relationship. The problem was he'd discover a new woman in every city. In every port of call, a new romance bloomed. He would then proceed to court her from afar, by text, email, and phone... until he traveled to a new city and fell for someone new. Each time we connected, he complained he wanted to find a person to share his life with, but by all accounts he was too busy hedging his bets, hiding one woman from the other's discovery. And he wondered why it was so difficult to fall for someone he really loved! His love life resembled a non-stop carousel of women. Then, it finally happened— the man who women seemed to go out of their way to be available for fell absolutely head-over-heels in love with a woman who loved him, but was psychologically and physically unavailable. She was married, and was too emotionally unstable to uproot her life for him. Heartbroken and alone, he was finally forced to confront how unfulfilling this self-created lifestyle was. The last I heard from him, he was still alone, but he was at peace. This brief heartbreaking relationship reinvigorated his spirit. He was spending more time with his kids from a previous marriage, and had become more introspective and interested in personal growth. He looked more content, less frenzied, more at peace than I'd ever seen him.

Lovers can stimulate the wild gypsy in our heart to finally break loose and discover ourselves—maybe for the first time. But living our relationship life solely from the fifth house eventually stunts our relationship growth. We may need to experience the experimentation, variety, and fun courtship that short-term sexual partnerships offer for a time, but we can never reach the fruits of intimacy by staying in a fifth house relationship. If the prospect of long-term intimacy and its sameness and responsibility sounds too scary or boring, we may be stuck in the fifth house, never leaving the dating merry-go-round. And until the day comes when intimacy and commitment is more exciting than spontaneity and romance, that's all there ever will be.

We don't have to take lover after lover; we can find many different ways to satisfy the urge for more spontaneous, spine-tingling moments in our lives. A fifth house planet may have a few love lessons to learn that are specific to that planet, but it also offers the potential for a rich, full, exciting creative life. By cultivating the art of total absorption and immersion in the present moment—by creating art, spending time with children, attending fun events, and making a place in our life for absorbing experiences of joyful spontaneity—we're less vulnerable to the shadowy aspect of the fifth house. And when we liberate that falling-in-love feeling of fascination, astonishment, absorption, and *joie de vivre* from being dependent on another person, we feel ageless, like a kid again.

There's No Shame in Short Term!

In America we have a clear preference for monogamous lifelong partnerships. Just ask anyone who is still single and in their forties! Unfortunately, this places a stigma on those people who share more than a bit of unfinished business with others, necessitating a higher number of short-term partners. If you have planets in the fifth house, you may share karmic business with a number of mates, which requires you to be free to mingle for a time, though you may feel social pressure to marry or commit. That's the beauty of knowing astrology. We can see that some people have more short-term partnerships than others. As long as we're being loving, self-aware, and growing, there is nothing wrong with having momentary mates. Every person in our life plays a precious role.

The Joys of Puddle Jumping

Always jump in the puddles! Always skip alongside the flowers. The only fights worth fighting are the pillow and food varieties. —Terri Guillemets

Children have neither past nor future; they enjoy the present, which very few of us do. —Jean de la Bruyère

What a distressing contrast there is between the radiant intelligence of the child and the feeble mentality of the average adult. —Sigmund Freud

The end of childhood is when things cease to astonish us. When the world seems familiar, when one has got used to existence, one has become an adult. —Eugene Ionesco

I still get wildly enthusiastic about little things. I play with leaves. I skip down the street and run against the wind. —Leo Buscaglia

A grownup is a child with layers on. —Woody Harrelson

There's a lot we leave behind in childhood, like unicorns and our imagination. One of the better things is the ability to spontaneously live in the wonder-filled present moment. Think about the last time you lost yourself for a while, so absolutely, happily absorbed in the present moment. You probably weren't thinking about "adult things." It's hard to worry about bills, wars, and politics when you're absorbed in catching tadpoles or a game of hopscotch. I remember summer afternoons as a kid spent roller skating. I'd get out my ghetto blaster, assign parts to all my playmates, and put on neighborhood shows. There was nothing better in the world. Then we grow up, and as Woody Harrelson says, we pile on the layers.

We forget what it's like to let loose and let go. To throw ourselves a roller-skating party, to make art that doesn't care a fig about critics, to be radiant and glorious and full of light—be it in our fairy and cowboy costumes or our birthday suit. This is what it means to be a kid, and there's a kid hiding in everyone's fifth house, whether you have a planet there or not. If your fifth house cusp is Aries (or contains Mars), working up a sweat, competitive games, and sports really gets your kid going. If your fifth house cusp is Capricorn (or contains Saturn), your kid enjoys being a little adult— mastering hobbies that seem grown-up or even dull to other kids makes Capricorn smile.

This is the house of recreation. Recreation is neither superfluous nor trivial. Think about the word. During recreation, astrologer Howard Sasportas said in his book *The Twelve Houses*, we are re-creating ourselves. We feel more alive during recreational activities that we enjoy because in the moments that we're utterly absorbed in our creative process, we are renewing our vital life force. Art-making, hobbies, performing, going to the ball game, knitting, or learning how to fly a plane—any creative, spontaneous, fun, sometimes even risky activity that allows us to lose ourselves, to get lost in the moment, and forget all those inhibitions we get really good at carrying around as adults also helps us find ourselves all over again.

Then there's sex. A benefit of not being a kid any longer: We get to have sex! Astrology traditionally says this is the house of recreational sex (versus the sexually committed intimacy of the eighth house). Sex with a partner can be incredibly deep, spiritual, and sacred—the kind of intimacy in which sexual desire is a vehicle for experiencing the transcendent together. That's eighth house sex. But sex can also be ego-strengthening and confidence-building. This is fifth house sex, which is less about soul-stirring enlightenment than feeling athletically, sexually attractive. As we discover how good this or that feels, we gain sexual confidence in the fifth house. Fifth house sex can be an affirmation that we have "it" going on.

The fifth house holds more than just our potential for shared karma—it holds a gamut of possibilities for creative fulfillment, along with specific guidance toward the type of spontaneous fun that will flame the lagging flames of passion in our romance (as explored in Section

3). What flames the fans of lagging passion like delving into the moment and having a little fun together?

Having randy sex, making mud pies, watching butterflies hatch, painting, making music, developing a creative hobby, and being a kid again all have a central thing in common: By dropping into the present moment, our life force is renewed. When we do these things, we release, recharge, and renew our vital energy body. A fifth house activity makes us feel like a kid again, and it does something else that is all too easy to forget in our modern, fast-paced, competitive, and future-oriented society: It reminds us that joy is found in the magic of the moment.

Playmates and Play Dates

Today you are You, that is truer than true. There is no one alive who is Youer than You. —Dr. Seuss

We all need playmates in life, and we can identify those playmates through our fifth house. Fifth house playmate relationships have a lively, playful quality. These people energize us; they have that special zip, zing, and pizazz that really gets us going. But behind all the fun, we are exchanging something valuable. The shared karma of our playmates may revolve around helping each other to cultivate a talent, or to step into the limelight of self-expression—professionally, creatively, or theatrically. At best, our playmates serve as creative catalysts. Their appearance in our lives, their presence, and who they are in the world can help us to self-actualize.

Self-actualization is a term that's been used by a variety of psychologically minded folks, but it was an organism scientist, Kurt Goldstein, who originated the idea. He described self-actualization as "the tendency to actualize, as much as possible, [the organism's] individual capacities." Imagine a butterfly becoming even truer to its butterfly nature. Self-actualization is the act and behavior of becoming truer to your unique self. As you actualize, you become more individual. More *You*.

In the birth chart, we self-actualize our entire chart through our Ascendant—located on the first house cusp of the birth chart—which strives to focus, organize, integrate, and present all of our different self-parts to the world in an authentic way. What does the fifth house have to do with the Ascendant/first house? They are connected by trine—an astrological aspect (or a geometrical relationship) indicating a facilitative and flowing connection. Our playmates, romantic or otherwise, support us; they want to help us shine. They facilitate something to occur in our lives by stimulating our confidence, leadership, and creativity. Their erotic attention and their belief in us arouses our ability to let our light shine, to take daring new risks.

Terri has planets Jupiter, Saturn, Venus (and asteroids Pallas and Juno*), all in the fifth house in Capricorn. Many of Terri's playmate relationships involve influential people—Capricorn is the sign of professional advancement and contributions to the community. At the beginning of her career, she became good friends with a mayor and his wife. This couple would invite her to their house for cocktail and dinner parties, and it was their professional friendship and realistic sage advice that helped her to navigate key career moves. At another time, she became friends with a superior court judge, with whom she attended many sporting events (sports being a fifth house activity) and about whom Terri said, "he just really got it" and "believed in me". Both men, Terri reported, had a great sense of mirth-making humor (Capricorn claims a high number of comedians to the sign), and both men died—one way of effectively ending an exchange.

Many were role models, helping Terri to claim her professional identity. Terri met a successful female attorney, whom she considers a Capricorn-type playmate, through a crafting circle (mythically, Pallas Athena, in addition to being the only female allowed into Roman court, also taught crafting!). Terri says of her friend: "We're not best friends; we don't call each other at critical life events and don't have those kind of expectations. But when my friend passes through town, we pick up right where we left off as though no time has passed." Friendships that feel special but aren't necessarily your best friends are fifth house playmates.

Terri believes she has had an above-average number of special relationships with fifth house playmates. She says they all "have a great sense of humor, help me to feel joy and pleasure, really have it together and they're tons of fun. Some of these relationships have had romantic erotic overtones, others do not". But all of her playmates have, just as the fifth house flows easily to the Ascendant, a catalytic and self-actualizing effect on her life path. Terri says, "My natal fourth house Sun is a bit reticent.

Through social events, days at the game, and parties, my playmates have drawn me outside of myself. Many of these relationships have been profound for me, though some have ended in various ways, but my special relationships are my true playmates in life. They have encouraged me to take the art of having fun seriously, and have caused me to grow in innumerable ways."

Is it possible to have a packed fifth house and still be in a committed partnership? Having opposite-sex playmates while in a committed partnership can challenge cultural taboos, or our partner's insecurities, but skillfully navigating those hairy edges can be deeply rewarding. Terri says, "Sometimes I do feel I'm crossing socially appropriate lines with my playmates. But then I recognize that I need these people in my life. They add dimensions to my life which I believe you can't expect one person to fulfill. I think that because of the nature of my relationship to my husband, I have an intensified need for these fifth house relationships. Sometimes these relationships are really intense. They've rocked my world by causing me to evaluate myself and re-evaluate my marriage—to look at what makes me truly happy, which has been invaluable to me, and also to my marriage."

We don't have to leave our playmates behind in the childhood schoolyard. Playmates validate our self-essence; they draw something special out of us. Like the childhood rhyme, "say, say oh playmate come out and play with me," your playmates invite you to open up and share yourself with them and the larger world. In moments of uninhibited sharing—over a cup of coffee, yoga class, guitar lesson, or knitting circle—playmates help you become "more Youer than You".

*Asteroids are not planets, and are not covered in this book. For more information, read *Asteroid Goddesses* by Demetra George.

Section 3

Planets and Signs through the Fifth House

While the fifth house describes a specific kind of shared relationship karma, the fifth house is not only the house of shared karma. If we have a planet here, there's also an evolutionary need to claim our talents and gifts symbolized by that archetype, and to impress our imaginative processes on the world in a creative way. Naturally ruled by the playful, expressive sign of Leo, a sign aligned with a need for fun, the renewal of spontaneity, a need to be noticed for one's creative expressions, planets and signs in the fifth house tell us how we do this, how to have a good time, play, and be a child again.

They may be preoccupied by romantic relationships, but someone with planets here will spend time and effort on doing something that to the rest of the world looks like fun—dating, creating, entertaining, socializing, and playing, to name a few. Many beloved entertainers have planets in the fifth house. For instance, Mick Jagger, Rod Stewart, and Carla Bruni, who all have Venus here, are as notorious for their artistry as their melodramatic love lives. Yet even if it looks like a scintillating hotbed of romantic activity and non-stop fun (as it should be!), this arena is a generator of both creative and karmic work.

In astrology, planets are energy, while signs describe motivation. People with fifth house planets simply have more energy to expend on fifth house activities, dating, and creating. Artistic genius Frida Kahlo had irreverent, innovative Uranus in her natal fifth house, and indeed during her time no one was making art (or love) quite like Frida. Frida's Uranus was in the hard working and "take me seriously" sign of Capricorn.

If you've got a fifth house planet, you've got something to give, to share with the world, in a way that only you can. You're meant to be putting yourself out there, taking risks, being creative, and growing through short-term partnerships. So dare to shine: Your fifth house planet is ready!

Before you begin reading about your planet or that of a loved one, you may want to read through these practical questions about the fifth house.

How can I identify my karmic mates using astrology?

As you read the descriptors, I suggest you look at your fifth house planet/sign as though it were a character starring in the play of your life. Don't limit yourself to romantic connections. Think about your playmates, creative catalysts, and "extras"—especially people with whom you shared special chemistry and who were in your life for a brief time. Consider your family and clan members, people you feel mysteriously bonded to. In family, we often sense we share a longer history than just this one lifetime. While it's impossible to know whether or not you share karma with someone, the accompanying text is meant to stimulate your imagination, not define your experience. Any relationship that carries a strong energetic charge is a candidate for a karmic mate.

Your description of my fifth house describes an aspect of my personality, but it also describes the character of my karmic mate and how to handle them. Does my fifth house planet describe me, or my karmic mate?

Both! Your fifth house contains your personal traits and karma related to your planet and sign, as well as the attributes of those with whom you will share a connection based around the exchange of the right use of will, in love. Even if it's your planet, stalled issues that need addressing may appear in either, or both, of you.

Is it possible to be affected by someone else's fifth house planetary energies—even if we don't have a planet here?

Absolutely! The fifth house describes *shared karma* and both partners do not need to have a fifth house planet to share karma. One's character, one's astrological makeup, need only resemble the other person's fifth house planet.

Let's say Nicole is in a romantic relationship with Katy, who has a fifth house Sun. Whenever they're out with friends, Katy notices that Nicole always seems to become the center of attention while she feels herself becoming increasingly invisible. Ever since Nicole suggested they move in together, Katy's feeling of being overshadowed by Nicole has become so preoccupying, that she doesn't know if she can remain in the relationship.

Katy has a fifth house planet; Nicole doesn't. However, Nicole is a Leo Sun, an outgoing, naturally attention-seeking "solar type", with a strong ego which activates Katy's fifth house. In other words, if you're partnered with someone who has a fifth house planet—*and especially if you strongly possess the character traits of their fifth house planet*—you may be scripted into the role of their fifth house planet. And vice versa.

This means if your mate has the Moon/Cancer in the fifth house, and you've got a strong Moon/Cancer in your chart, or your mate has Mars/Aries in the fifth house and Mars/Aries is strong in your makeup (and so on), you are a prime candidate for working out shared karma.

What can the fifth house tell me about romance?

We initially experience a fifth house buzz in all relationships, yet as we establish the bond that zing starts to incrementally wane as the intention of our relationship makes itself known. As such, the fifth house describes the energy field we experience when we first meet. It gives us that zip, zap, zing when we first meet someone special, but it also suggests behaviors and activities we can cultivate to spice things up in the long term.

What if I'm in a long-term relationship? What can the fifth house teach me?

The fifth house alerts us to how to renew the romance and get the spark back in a relationship that needs spicing up. Use the information you learn about your fifth house to raise your energy field, to bring the pizazz back.

What if I feel I have karmic mates, but I have no planet in the fifth house?

Planet(s) here bring more action, energy, and karmic mates to this area of life, but if you don't have a planet here, read for the sign on the fifth house cusp. You may be surprised by how much your sign can tell you about your short-term partners, and your creative and romantic energy. Also, you might want to consider that you have partnered with a person/people who has/have a fifth house planet, thus sharing karma in that way.

What if I have more than one planet in my fifth house?

The more planets you have here, the more fifth house lessons and shared karma you have in this lifetime. Read for them all. You may find the description of all your fifth house planets describes a multidimensional playmate or karmic mate, or you may find that one person resembles your one planet, another person carries your second or third planet, and so on.

My fifth house (or fifth house ruler) is being transited. What can I expect?

If the fifth house ruler or a planet in the fifth house is receiving a transit (including by progression or solar arc), this is a highly creative and potentially surprising time. Karmic mates can come out of the woodwork as shared karma between two people makes itself known. Children may enter the picture, or dominate your energy and focus. Latent talents may develop. Your pleasure center is being stimulated during this time, but should you meet someone who rocks your world, consider keeping your romantic attachments loose and orienting yourself towards finishing up old business. Enjoy the wild ride!

Sun in the Fifth, or Leo on the Cusp: The King or Queen

A day without sunshine can make even the most good-natured person glum. When the Sun shines, we feel happier, more confident and capable. Likewise, the astrological Sun is the energy body that radiates vitality, will, and charisma, and a person born with a fifth house Sun has had prior lifetime(s) where their solar spontaneity, will, and self-expression were squelched. On the playbill for this life: Getting noticed! Being seen! Taking up space! Since this squelching could have created a condition of insecurity or fear of getting noticed for the fifth house Sun person, fun, play, creative expression, and being a kid again are all excellent ways to coax the Sun person out from behind the shadows and into the limelight, where he or she rightfully belongs.

The Sun is the center of our solar system and the center of our universe. The Sun takes up space, literally, and just as humans have worshipped the Sun God for millennia, this person needs to be noticed and seen. And a little fun-loving worship, relationally, goes a long way with them, as good-humored worshippers in the form of a fan club or a number-one fan will encourage their inner largesse to come out and play, express, shine. Encouragement to self-express, and the accompanying affection that comes from this, isn't just important for these people—it's karmic medicine, a balm for having experienced lifetimes of standing in the shadows.

A fifth house Sun needs its proper "day in the Sun". If this is you, take the center stage. Pick up a paintbrush or pen, play the piano, dance. Live in the center of your own life. Choose to play the lead role: Run for mayor, start your own business, become the leader of your local environmental group. Do what inspires passion and love in you, because when you lead with your heart, others will gladly follow. Most importantly, don't play second fiddle to those who lead from ego instead of the heart.

Your karmic mate... has a natural presence, charisma, gravity, and leadership ability; may be self-centered or narcissistic.

Imagine two kids, Bobby and Ricky, both running for class president. There they sit in the cafeteria lunchroom, each holding a popularity contest at their respective tables. Both have a number of friends and fans, but it's a horse race. They eye one another, two competitors vying for a leadership role... when Ricky lobs a milk carton onto Bobby's table. Bobby starts doubting himself. *Maybe*, he thinks, *I'm just not up for the task.*

When it comes down to it, kid lunchroom politics aren't so different from that of adults. Solar fifth house karma involves being threatened by another person's gravity, charisma, and authority. Their charisma overpowers us. Their authority may obscure ours. We land our dream job only to realize our boss is like a dimmer switch that's constantly turning down, minimizing our light and our efforts. We work up the nerve to enter the talent show, and someone upstages us. Why is this happening? In a nutshell, no one is better at helping us learn that we have a right to exist and take up space than someone who is exceedingly comfortable at doing exactly that.

In an ongoing relationship, the nature of shared Sun karma revolves around two people claiming their respective right to be leaders and creative individuals, while neither person outshines the other. Two Sun Kings (or Sun Queens) must learn to live and rule together under the same sky without feeling threatened by the other. Attempts to outshine the other will only create animosity and competitiveness, a bickering of two leaders.

Creativity, art, performance, and children all belong to the domain of the fifth house. For the fifth house Sun, putting oneself out there—for a project, business, skill, craft, or hobby—empowers a sense of specialness and vitality. Children are natural generators of the joy and aliveness that the youthful Sun craves, so having kids of their own, or working with them, is a no-brainer for these people. The Sun in the fifth craves a physical manifestation of their creative self-expression, a "creative baby" that reflects them, so children often fit that bill. Though there can be a tendency to live through their children, the Sun person feels fulfilled by simply having creative progeny, both artistic and/or biological.

Is there enough room for two Suns in the galaxy? Can we sustain an ongoing relationship with a mate who shares solar karma with us? There are people who have elected to do just that. Many famous fifth house Sun people share fifth house karma with their mates. Katie Holmes, a fifth house (Sagittarius) Sun married Tom Cruise, a charismatic personality whose attention-getting antics almost eclipsed Oprah. Yoko Ono, an Aquarian, was married to John Lennon; Anaïs Nin (Pisces Sun) to Henry Miller; Priscilla Presley, a Gemini, to Elvis (quite literally, the King - of Rock 'n' Roll)... all were born with a fifth house Sun, and all had powerful partners who could've easily overshadowed them, potentially causing the fifth house Sun person to doubt their self.

Fifth house Sun people often partner with charismatic and magnetic people by whom anyone could feel dominated. They may indeed need the solar leadership of their karmic mate *to goad them into shining as brightly as they're capable.* Disappear under the sunbeams of their King or Queen mate? They simply cannot! For instance, after divorcing Tom Cruise, Katie Holmes started a second career on Broadway and has never looked happier. She's finally herself again.

In summary, mates with whom you need to finish business may:

-Attempt to dominate, overshadow, or outshine you.

-Refuse to recognize your creative contributions or your creative identity.

-Be threatened by your charisma, talent, authority, or leadership.

- Help you to: develop your leadership abilities, own your talents, express yourself, and step into your power.

If you have Sun in the fifth house: You deserve to shine in your own right. Humans worshipped the Sun God for a reason: you were born to get noticed.

If you are in a relationship with a fifth house Sun: Be their number one fan. Support, share, and appreciate their creative projects, but first and foremost encourage them to step up, out, and be their own person. Recognize that you may cast a large shadow; be wary of situations that create competition between both of you.

Your required romantic chemistry for a mate:

-Charisma, confidence, honor, spontaneity, talent, and leadership.

-Someone who is worthy of others' praise, and able to share the limelight with you.

-Mutual admiration. You see a playmate who can hold his or her own, and they see the same in you.

Your playmates and creative catalysts are: Natural leaders, influential people, god or goddess-like, Kings, Queens, performers, VIPs.

To renew the spark of passion: Attend a play, show, or VIP event. Have a lavish night on the town. Eat dinner at a five-star restaurant. Play King (or Queen) for a day, your lover as willing subject, then switch roles.

Fifth house Sun notables: Katie Holmes, Wolfgang Amadeus Mozart, Leonardo da Vinci, Marilyn Manson, Marie Antoinette, Nicolas Sarkozy, Yoko Ono, Franklin D. Roosevelt, Marlene Dietrich, Priscilla Presley, Louis Armstrong, Anaïs Nin, J.R.R. Tolkien, Malcolm X, Bette Davis, Jim Jones, Aretha Franklin, Alexander McQueen.

Moon in the Fifth, or Cancer on the Cusp: The Crowd Pleaser

Kids are notorious hams. Attention-getters who create dances, plays, finger paintings, and slapstick comedy better than any comedy hour, children haven't yet developed the inhibitions that adults eventually do, making them experts at having fun. Yet play is a legitimate human need! In this regard, the fifth house Moon person never really grows up. Why should they want to? In sharp contrast to dreary adulthood, childhood is full of fairy wings, unicorns, and gladiators.

The Moon is the planet of romance, imagination, and illusion. Having no light of its own, it reflects the light of the Sun amplifying the creative, fun-loving, and artistic energies of the fifth house. With their natural imagination and love for romance, in terms of what can be created, the sky's the limit. Natural entertainers who are able to simultaneously creatively express what others are feeling, and help others to feel comfort and ease, unlike the Sun, they usually find it easy to be the center of attention. Even if the childhood was less than ideal, a fifth house Moon person's innate sense of specialness was likely nurtured along the way, allowing their talents and artistry to uninhibitedly, spontaneously come forth.

For the Moon, ideal friends and lovers are eager and indulgent audience members, hungry for the jokes, whimsical interests, and spontaneous hijinks that the fifth house Moon continually dishes up. If the fifth house Moon missed out on the chance we all need as children— to be the center of attention, the apple of someone's eye— the healing method is spontaneous self-expression of the feelings of life and imagination. The fifth house Moon's emotional life often resembles Greek theater. Where feelings of joy and sorrow spontaneously flow, emotional memories of being neglected or ignored are washed away by tears and laughter. Each time they spontaneously and soulfully express, their heart is a little more healed.

Your karmic mate... is naturally nurturing or maternal; may not be able to separate you as an individual from his or her needs and wants for you.

There's nothing like the unconditional love of family, but even the love of a dear mother can be crippling (just ask Norman Bates!). Even a good parent, "only wanting what's best for us", can suffocate us with their able steering and guidance. Family unfortunately also tends to freeze us in time. We may forever remain "little Jonny," "mom", or "wife." In family, we're often treated as an extension of others' wants, desires, and needs for us.

Shared Moon karma revolves around being seen exclusively as an extension of someone else's biological or emotional needs at the expense of being seen as a multi-faceted human being. We've all had moments when, examining the weathered pages of the family photo album, we came across a beautiful, dignified young person and incredulously thought: "*That* was mom (or dad)?" We knew them as our parent; sadly, we never really knew *them*. Transpose this onto an adult relationship and things get sticky, and potentially codependent. When human beings are reduced to a role or expectation, it robs them of their dignity, individuality, and independence. This is the karma seeking resolution.

To resolve it, we must walk that fine line between providing, loving, and supporting unconditionally, and giving each other room to grow. This is the house of children, so in addition to two people who share children, parents and their children can also share a karmic contract. It's logical to see the other person in a specific role, but we must learn to give the person wings in these relationships. With Moon here, we might unconsciously ask a partner to stay the same person he or she was when we first married or dated, or to fulfill traditional housewife or breadwinner roles—roles our parents played (or likewise, be asked to fulfill those requests for another). When independence is sacrificed for the couple or family, Moon karma can lead to codependence. Too unconscious, too afraid to break the expectations accompanying relationship roles, we neglect to claim our personhood and, sadly, forfeit the right to an identity. If claiming freedom to grow within the partnership is not possible, the contract may need to end.

Fifth house Moon people often possess an urge to start their own biological family; their karmic mate will usually share that drive, too. Having children can be one of life's greatest joys, yet throughout history many important things have been sacrificed for that joy: dreams, passions, independence. With the Moon here, there's also the danger of a couple becoming so focused on the needs of the family that they forget their own needs as humans and lovers. This tendency happens with startling ease in family units. A father of two told me that if something happens to be bothering him or his partner, concern about their children or making plans for the children's week tend to create "an escape hatch, so we don't have to talk to each other about our real feelings".

Children and childhood—with its copious opportunities for creative whimsy—occupy the imaginations of fifth house Moon people. Performer Britney Spears has Moon (in Aquarius) in the fifth house. According to her mother, she began dancing and singing as soon as she could walk, and by eleven years old, she was performing, living up to the fifth house Moon's easy ability to connect with the public, opening hearts with their artistic expressiveness. Yet the Moon rules our irrational side, and for a long period of time the only pictures we saw of Britney were of a young, tear-streaked girl in overemotional, loony states. Britney also briefly married then divorced Kevin Federline, with whom she co-parents their children.

In an extreme example of the Moon's potential for codependency and dysfunction, famed porn star Linda Lovelace (Moon in Taurus) says she was lured into porn by a neighborhood friend who effectively made her a dependent by giving gifts and money to her impoverished family (and who later became her pimp, husband and abuser).

In summary, mates with whom you need to finish business may:

-See you as an extension of a role, not a whole human being.

-Need to be dependent on you, or make you dependent on them.

-Refuse to let you grow, or give you freedom to grow.

If you have Moon in the fifth house: Be a kid again, feel the hunger for play and the joy of doing what you love for the simple sake of enjoying yourself.

If you are in a relationship with a fifth house Moon: Expect to have fun, creativity, and whimsy on the menu, as fifth house Moon folks love to have a good time! Watch out for self-sacrifice: there's a good chance either/both of you ask the other to give up too much in the name of family, children, or partnership.

Your required romantic chemistry for a mate:

-Emotional openness and expressiveness.

-One who encourages vulnerability, tenderness, laughter.

-They indulge your inner child, but don't treat you as a child.

Your playmates and creative catalysts are: Mother figures, children, women, natural nurturers, therapists, healers, poets, romantics.

To renew the spark of passion: Passion is all too easily replaced by the assumed familiarity of shared biological roles for the Moon, so it's important to support one another's individuality, creative choices, desires, whimsies, and need for independence from the partnership. Support one another's inner child by asking their kid what they want, and then indulge them!

Fifth house Moon notables: Britney Spears, Gordon Ramsay, Ernest ("Papa") Hemingway, Al Pacino, Pablo Picasso, Grace Kelly, Ben Affleck, Steven Spielberg, Michael Moore, Andrea Bocelli, John Malkovich, Ringo Starr, Linda Lovelace, Barbra Streisand, Sri Aurobindo.

Mercury in the Fifth, or Gemini/Virgo on the Cusp: The Conversationalist

Imagine being entertained by your favorite storyteller or author—an entertaining orator you want to listen to, hear, and watch, for their words have heft, weight, and authority. They are interesting to listen and talk to. They may have a way with words, be exceptionally intelligent, gifted in language arts, or have a special way of connecting from the heart. Those born with Mercury in the fifth house rejoice in the art of self-expression. They are the acquaintance who sidles up to you with a wisecrack at the PTA meeting you've been long-dreading, the salesman who phoned you on a bad day but gently humors you to the point of warmth and friendship.

A fifth house Mercury person needs to feel the impact of his or her voice on others. In the karmic past, their voice went unheard and unnoticed. Now, like a singer serenading a crowd or a stand-up comedian, he or she feeds off the energy of an eager, appreciative audience. Sharing news bits, relaying entertaining stories, and getting a feel for their ideas and thoughts, without needing to come up with an ultimate answer, empowers self-expression. Weaving different disciplines of thought together, revolutionizing and cross-pollinating ideas about culture and politics, art and sciences, Mercury is happily humming and expressing what it loves: gathering data, then passing the torch of knowledge to others.

Mercury karma revolves around the art of language, intelligence, and communication. Karmically, this person may be intimidated or insecure in his or her own voice, believing others have more authority, intelligence, and knowledge, thus leading the Mercury person to relinquish his or her voice, perceptions, and intelligence. The remedy? To speak one's mind! To dare to voice opinions, thoughts, and ideas—and do it with heart.

Your karmic mate is... smart, witty, cunning, looks good on paper, may be immature or deceptive.

Someone wise once said: the ears may listen, but it's the heart that hears. If we had only one communication tool, listening with and speaking from the heart would be enough. Without heart, the wise ones also say, "Talk is cheap", because it's not grounded in the heart's wisdom.

The Mercury person's shared karma involves effectively, honestly, and appropriately *speaking and listening*. This implies a previous blockage in two-way communication, of one or both partners not being forthright in communication—listening, but not actually hearing the other, speaking from the head and not the heart, having one's self-expression or intelligence trivialized.

Mercury is the planet of intelligence, but when intelligence is an ego-attribute, it can block us from truly connecting. If you've ever watched a trial lawyer, you know words can be tricky. People can bend the truth to their advantage and tongue-tie others with clever, winning arguments—even if that argument is wrong. Strategies like monopolizing the conversation so that no one else gets a word in edgewise, or analyzing another's logic or rationale to death, create huge barriers to flowing two-way communication, and often block it altogether. In authentic heart-driven communication, there's no need to use fancy words or show your credentials to justify your thoughts. No one needs to be "smart enough" to have their voice valued and respected by others.

Intelligence is attractive to, and romantically stimulating for, Mercury in the fifth. The parents and family members often also prize intellectual aptitude. A fifth house Mercury client of mine was born into a wealthy Ivy

League family where intellectual prowess was the barometer for success. This influenced her choice of partner—everyone she dated had to look impressive on paper to the family first. Another acquaintance (with Gemini on the cusp) came from a blue-collar background and married into a family of lawyers and doctors where intellectual achievement was prize, which in his case, positively motivated him to seek higher education and pursue a career in the sciences. They eventually divorced, their karma around higher education, exchanged.

With this karma, we may become so enamored of another's novel wit, mind, intelligence, or youthful cleverness, that we are willing to overlook the fact that a mate is less than honest, truthful, or forthcoming—until it's too late and the relationship's trust is compromised. Our Mercury mate may resemble the youthful, clever Trickster archetype. We meet a person who refuses to grow up, who tricks others (and us) with his or her playfulness, who lies, who bends or outright disobeys the rules. In myth, as a young babe Mercury snuck out of his bassinet and stole Apollo's sacred cattle. When caught, he charmed and sweet-talked his way out of the whole mess. The Mercury mate can have a silver tongue, talking his or her way into and out of situations, and coming out smelling like roses. A dark Mercury character can get away with murder—but only if we let them!

Shared Mercury karma teaches us the importance of clear communication and builds confidence in expressing our intellectual acumen and perceptions. But since Mercury is vulnerable to people who tell a good story but don't have their facts straight, these gifts may have to be learned the hard way—by falling for someone who, at best, is less than straightforward and has poor communication skills; or, at worst, is skilled at deception. For those born with Mercury here, picking up on the subtleties of communication is a necessary skill. It can make all the difference between spending time with a trustworthy person, versus one who is not.

In summary, mates with whom you need to finish business may:
-Be more interested in listening to themselves talk than in getting to know you.
-Be youthful, immature, deceptive, tricky, scattered.
-Be disconnected from their own heart wisdom.

If you have Mercury in the fifth house: From books, to modern art, to what makes the sky blue, there are so many things to talk about and teach. Open up and share your voice. People want to hear what you have to say, so go ahead and say it.

If you are in a relationship with a fifth house Mercury: Restless, young at heart, and perpetually craving variety and stimulation, your Mercury mate will keep you interested, and in stitches! Either/both of you need to develop a B.S. meter. When truthful topics are being evaded, work on communicating from the heart.

Your required romantic chemistry for a mate:
-An open-minded conversationalist who can talk about a wide variety of topics.
-A person with whom you share wit, verbal rapport, curiosity, humor.
-Is expressive, but curious about your thoughts and wants to know what you think.

Your playmates and creative catalysts are: Teachers, networkers, writers, reporters, thinkers.

To renew the spark of passion: Try texting, emailing, love letters, and ingenious inventions like fortune cookie love notes placed in unexpected places.

Avoid what Mercury most dreads, *boredom,* through spontaneous trips, classes. Keep things fresh. Mercury romance relies on the new and novel every single day.

Fifth house Mercury notables: Steve Jobs, Marlon Brando, Tiger Woods, Tyra Banks, Russell Brand, Wolfgang Amadeus Mozart, Victor Hugo, Michael J. Fox, Diana Ross, Julie Delpy, Joni Mitchell, Bill Maher, Mae West, Charlie Chaplin, RuPaul, Larry Flynt, Vanessa Redgrave, Federico Fellini, Jim Jones.

Venus in the Fifth, or Libra/Taurus on the Cusp: The Temptress

Just as every little girl dreamed of becoming Venus, the otherworldly beauty and seductress who could have anyone she wanted, every little boy wanted her on his arm. Venus is dreamy for a reason. When we are under the shining, diamond-like beam of Venus' attentions, the world takes on new color. Through her eyes, our ordinary life becomes inspired, enchanting. Under her erotic gaze, we even become more desirable to our own eyes.

Someone wise once said, "Beautiful people are easy to love." For a fifth house Venus, there is something about meeting a sexy, sensual, desirable person that compels the excitement of instant affection, rapport, and connection. And that's where trouble walks through the front door. Those with Venus in the fifth house are primed to meet a few heavenly creatures in their lifetime, and even fall in love with them. But when it comes to committed love, a sexy, desirable, exciting mate is only the first box we should tick off on a long questionnaire. While the fifth house cocktail of desire is necessary for a connection to initially spark, when it comes to how two people will actually fare in a long-term commitment—a union anchored in self and mutual understanding, trust, humility, empathy, maturity—the fifth house falls silent.

We all sell ourselves at the outset of a romance, showing only our best and most attractive face. We want to be loved, adored, desired, and eroticized in another's eyes. Those with Venus here must actively seek the authentic person in front of them; they must learn to look beyond appearances and into the other's hidden side—his or her craziness, dysfunction, madness, and humanity. After a few heartaches, she may start to wisely regard any love prospects with a chaotic, messy relationship history with caution and an instinct for self-preservation. When Venus develops the eyes to see past the veneer and into the person in front of her, warts and all, she can enter a relationship with open eyes. Then she's free to simply enjoy Venus' partnering gifts, the joy of sharing spontaneous chemistry with a variety of charming, inspiring mates who help her feel erotically alive.

Your karmic mate is... attractive, sophisticated, smooth, slick, has a chaotic relationship history, and is potentially manipulative.

We all wear blinders when we fall in love, initially, but the fifth house Venus person has a hard time taking them off long enough to discern romantic mates from lifelong partners. Rod Stewart, who has Venus (Pisces) in the fifth house, alluded to this when he said, "Instead of getting married again, I'm going to find a woman I don't like and just give her a house." For those with this placement, there's often a necessary and missing distinction to make between people whom one should date or marry. But Mick Jagger—Venus (Virgo) here— tried to have it all when, while married to Jerry Hall, he fathered a child with a Brazilian model, Luciana Morad. This wasn't his first indiscretion. Even his masseuse was quoted as saying, "He looks like an old raisin but he's still wicked sexy. He has this giant Grand Canyon ego and it just can't be filled by one woman." (Astrodatabank.com)

Like Stewart and Jagger, fifth house Venus-born can have chaotic, messy relationship lives with all the romantic drama of Aphrodite herself. Infamous for her love exploits and being sexually self-possessed, we often forget that Venus was married. The mythical Greek Aphrodite (Venus) was a passion-loving, glamorous, and sensual creature who was betrothed to Hephaestus, a disabled forge smith who had a great talent for making things. He dearly loved her despite her continued affairs with his far more exciting, physically desirable brother, Ares. Aphrodite may have been a lover of lustful Ares, but she *married* Hephaestus, a loyal, steadfast man with underrepresented talents—and flaws. In her marriage partner, we see a meeting of opposites, a marriage of complements. Aphrodite was glamorous, beautiful, and desirable; Hephaestus was not. In her marriage partner, we see someone who has been forged in the fires of his own humanity. As a fifth house Venus learns: the partners he or she find the most sexually and superficially desirable aren't often marriage material!

In shared karma, bonds need to be finished that revolve around exchanging creative and erotic energy—but this time, without the Venus veneer of mistaking a person for a life partner. A client of mine, Steve, with Venus here (Capricorn), finds himself constantly attracted to artists. A novice artist himself, he craves what he describes as "muse energy". Yet one is never just "the artist," and as other dimensions of their personality emerges - wounding, trust issues, mental instability, in his case- the projection eventually falls away, as it must.

Romantic love is deeply ingrained in this person's romantic partnering style, but intimacy is a multi-dimensional love that allows for the unconditional acceptance of faults, flaws, and humanity. Jungian analyst Robert Johnson once said, "One of the great paradoxes of romantic love is that it never produces human relationships as long as it stays romantic." To truly love another, the Venus person must allow that person to fall off the pedestal, to truly see and meet each other's imperfect wholeness. Like the story of Hephaestus and Aphrodite (and her lover, Ares), Venus needs both passion and humanity. When she finds this in the arms of one warm-blooded body, two people can fully enjoy the bounty of Aphrodite's pleasure gardens.

In summary, mates with whom you need to finish business may:

-Be materialistic, one-dimensional, seductresses or Casanovas.

-Have a messy, chaotic relationship history.

-Help you learn to see past romantic projection and idealization.

If you have Venus in the fifth house: Make it sweet, sugary, and cherry-flavored. You are here to experience the fun-loving, playful side of romantic partnership. Indulge. Have dessert first. Turn your romantic entanglements into beautiful art. That's how love songs are written.

If you are in a relationship with a fifth house Venus: You are in for a treat, as your Venus lover will put you on a pedestal and treat you like a God or Goddess. Either/both of you tend to idealize your partner, so let them see your flawed human side before one of you falls off and shatters the precious illusion.

Your required romantic chemistry for a mate:

-Has verve, creativity, artistry, style, sophistication.

-Enjoys a 50/50, democratic partnering style.

-Is relaxing, fun, pleasant to be around, and likes pleasing you as much as pleasing themselves.

Your playmates and creative catalysts are: Artists, lovers, diplomats, counselors, muses, creative types.

To renew the spark of passion: Venus rules those tangible and intangible rewards that make our life better: love, art, beauty, sweet indulgences, and laughter. In modern life, stress is the biggest obstruction to enjoying Venus' pleasures. Relaxation, getting enough sleep, doing things you deeply love and enjoy give you the sparkle you need to reignite your inner Temptress.

Fifth house Venus notables: Carla Bruni Sarkozy, Mick Jagger, Rod Stewart, Barack Obama, Bill Gates, Princess Diana, Prince William, George Harrison, Colin Farrell, Tina Turner, Marie Antoinette, Charlotte Gainsbourg, Melanie Griffith, Walt Disney, Natassaja Kinski, Yoko Ono, Franklin D. Roosevelt, Joseph Campbell.

Mars in the Fifth, or Aries on the Cusp: The Warrior

Picture your favorite action hero as a kid. There was no doubt a villain involved, a character who foiled your hero's attempts at justice. Mars sees the world as full of heroes and villains, enemies and victors. It's a polarized way of seeing, but we do live in a world of duality, and we make these black or white deductions about people all the time. We say we love our neighbor—until he puts his trash on our curb over and over again, or trespasses our person or property, at which point he becomes the enemy and Mars, the Warrior, is marshaled into action.

It's nice to think that about loving thy neighbor, but that's diplomatic Venus, not self-interested Mars. A fifth house Mars-born has heated encounters with mates, people who bring out his or her fire and anger. What will they do with that hot, uncomfortable energy? They could take revenge on their littering neighbor by sneaking out in the middle of the night and cutting down their prized roses. They could misdirect the energy and yell at their partner, kids, or dog. Or they could find healthy outlets for their aggression, ambition, and drive. The resolution of Mars karma relies on the *right use of will* regarding the expression of anger and sexuality with others.

Those born with fiery Mars in the flamboyant fifth house have moxie. They may not always be graceful about it, but they step up to the plate. Natural competitors, whether playing a game of marbles or sussing out the sale rack at Nordstrom's, in Mars' world there are only winners and losers, hunters and prey, victims and rebels. How to be a winner with Mars? Directly engage him. Be courageously honest. Be willing to take on a challenge. Goals help. Every hero needs a noble goal. Fighting for children's rights, teaching inner city kids basketball, changing the world through good nutrition—any activity that channels energy into productive movement helps. Working up a sweat helps, too. From tango to making love... for Mars, it matters less how you do it, and more that you just *do it*.

Your karmic mate is... formidable and fierce, may trespass boundaries, anger you, or push your buttons. They call on your courage, get you fired up.

Imagine a partnership in which one partner calls all the shots, while the more passive, forbearing partner relinquishes their will, resigning their opinions and choices to the more assertive partner. For many of us, this is easy to imagine; for instance, the stereotypical 1950s housewife, or the browbeaten husband. Throughout most of history, it has been men who domineered and steered the relationship, while women conceded and acquiesced, though women are just as capable of being the dominator. In a nutshell, we can impress our will onto a loved one, we can overrule and bulldoze, but that's not love, that's wilfulness.

Over time, what happens to the energy and confidence of a person who has been dominated by another? When the tension of holding back honesty, anger, ferocity and courage builds, that tension demands release. It's imperative that Mars-born have healthy outlets for offloading hot energy. Anger issues are a potential problem. The expression of anger is a shadowy fellow in our culture. Those who believe "I have a right to express my feelings" will unload their toxic emotions onto sensitive others, which is a violation of personal boundaries and space. Hot Mars energy needs to be made conscious, released, expressed in healthy, often physical ways. Physical outlets, like sports, dance, help release pent up energy. Mars aggression grows dangerous when it's out of control or unconscious, when we're unaware that we even have aggression or anger. Though the latter is usually not a problem for a fifth house Mars person, for whom warrior energy is usually expressed quite openly—even if sometimes too openly!

Mars isn't all strife and conflict, especially not in the fifth house. A fifth house Mars is playful, spirited and sporty, though love and romance may be their most favorite sport of all. After all, Mars was the sexy paramour to Love Goddess Venus, and in the fifth house Mars' virility and sexual libido is strong. The Mars person enjoys sexual conquests, regarding sex as fun, a form of pleasurable recreation and release rather than an expression of romantic intimacy or fidelity. Not one to hold back, if Mars wants to woo you, they do it with drama, color, and flair. Mars will impress you with a spontaneous trip to Vegas, organizing a bungee jump, or renting out an entire restaurant on your first date. If you're the object of Mars' affections, this doesn't mean they want to marry you—it's simply their romantic style.

Introverts may be initially attracted to Mars' dashing heroics, enthusiasm, and panache, but only those who can spar with Mars—keeping up with their verbal and sexual athletics and playful arguing banter—wins their heart for all time. The Mars person enjoys an equally strong-willed partner who can stand up for themselves and tolerate their sometimes demanding, competitive, and spontaneous nature. A warrior needs a worthy opponent.

This Mars loves playing the heroic protagonist, in both love and life. The word *protagonist* is Greek in origin, and translates as "first struggler" or "first important actor". The Mars person is working with his or her demonstrable "me first" energy and power to make things happen in the world. In order to feel charged up and alive, they need to express their robust life energy in playful, goal-driven, creative, and sometimes fierce ways. Woe to those who try to block this person's path!

Mythically, Mars was both lover and fighter, and the fifth house placement strengthens Mars' capacity for both courageous action, and passionate devotion to a lover or cause. A balance to the eleventh house of love received, the fifth is the house of love given. "Act only from love," this Mars suggests, "and all will be well". Shared Mars karma revolves around two people redeeming their personal code of honor, courage, and dignity through direct and honest confrontation, which, if done rightly, strengthens both people's sense of identity and power in the world. Then, standing in love, speaking from love, and acting from love, Mars can be a *warrior of love*.

In summary, mates with whom you need to finish business may:
-Make you angry, trespass your boundaries, oppose your will.
-Have unresolved anger/rage issues.
-Put you in touch with your anger, heat, sexuality.

If you have Mars in the fifth house: Release your hot energy through play, and recreational and creative activities that encourage you to face your fears and feel courageous and strong (without being foolhardy or reckless). Athletic activities, dancing, kung fu; anything that gets you moving helps you to move anger and fear out of your body and flexes your confidence muscle.

If you are in a relationship with a fifth house Mars: Romance and courageous daring go hand in hand for Mars, so prepare to be wowed by their intensity and enterprising appetite. One or both of you will be challenged to kindly respect and honor the other, while standing up for yourself. When tempers flare, learn how to "fight fairly" (in Charlotte Kasl's book, *If The Buddha Married*, a strategy for handling couples' conflict).

Your required romantic chemistry for a mate:
-Honesty, candor, directness.
-Possesses a sense of adventure and risk.
-Challenges you at times, but doesn't dominate you.

Your playmates and creative catalysts are: Champions, warriors, competitors, heroes, freedom fighters, athletes.

To renew the spark of passion: Feeling dull? A sense of adventure revives your romance to passionate heights. A trip to the Amazon rainforest or a climb to the top of Mount Everest is thrilling, but any physical activity that turns you on, and turns them on, and well... you can figure out the rest.

Fifth house Mars notables: Mel Gibson, Michael Moore, Serena Williams, Gordon Ramsay, George Clooney, Pamela Anderson, Jack Nicholson, Christopher Reeve, Kesha, Sigourney Weaver, Demi Moore, Dr. Dre,

Karl Marx, Martha Stewart, Vladimir Nabokov, Dorothy Parker.

Jupiter in the Fifth, or Sagittarius on the Cusp: The Bon Vivant

Imagine having your mind blown by a panoramic view of space, thousands of miles from Earth; or imagine receiving the expansive generosity of a gospel choir during Sunday morning church service. Imagine feeling generously blessed from meeting a profound spiritual teacher with true Buddha presence. What do all of these experiences have in common? You walk away feeling happier, lighter, more expansive, and more open. You leave these people and places feeling far more benevolent toward life, God, and the world than when you first arrived. You're more inclined to see the world optimistically, as an abundant, blessed place of full possibility.

You are ready to grow through the archetype of expansion, faith, and possibility. The soul intent of your fifth house Jupiter is to optimistically feast at the buffet of life. This includes entertaining new ways of thinking, seeing, and being in the world. This could also mean you are ready to express yourself in a more colorful and big way. Nurture your hobbies and artistic interests. Jupiter here favors sports and speculation, and when you take a gamble on yourself, you have luck on your side. Think of Jupiter as you would your favorite aunt or uncle, the one you know will always be on your side. Follow your wanderlust, curiosities, and yearnings. Take a leap of faith and the universe is especially indulgent with you.

The Jupiter person is just dying to dance on tables, buy that ticket to India, or purchase that astrology session. So let them! While a moralistic, negative, or miserly attitude will take the wind right out of the Jupiter person's sails, the right playmate and partner will introduce new vistas, encouraging Jupiter to explore and expand their world.

Your karmic mate is... generous, positive, philosophical, spiritual, and may promise more than he or she can realistically deliver.

Bon vivant means "one who lives well." What does it mean to you to live well? It could mean having money, a house in the nice part of town, someone to love, or a rich spiritual life. When we live the good life, we know we are blessed and abundant. We feel rich no matter what our circumstances are, because living well is an attitude.

Shared Jupiter karma can be quite lovely; we are enriched and uplifted by another's presence. We are shown favor by VIPs, and these important, worldly, and perhaps even famous people elevate our status in the world and help us grow in confidence. Jupiter is the archetype of the King, and friends of the King always receive generous gifts and perks. Shared Jupiter karma can create special opportunities. We receive—or if we are in the fortunate position to offer, we give another status, favor, specialness, privilege, and material, spiritual, and emotional support. Through the Jupiter relationship, we are substantially improved in life for a time.

Yet Jupiter isn't all special passes and VIP lounges. Jupiter here can incline us towards destructive habits of excess, and more to the point, relationships that support those habits. Janis Joplin had a fifth house Jupiter. She walked through her gypsy life wearing a mash-up of floppy hats, big sunglasses, bell bottoms, a messy swirl of color and largesse, reflecting the larger-than-life force of Jupiter. A woman with an appetite for life, Janis enjoyed drugs a little too much, overdosed, and died of "excess".

Shared Jupiter karma can also revolve around overestimating another person. Spiritual people often have this experience with their guru or teacher. A guru makes a mistake and the student is shocked, disillusioned to discover he or she is a human being with faults and failings, just like them. Jupiter in the fifth can do this with people they date, too. Seeing their love interest as a catch or a prize (and indeed they may be), they overlook important details and miss out on the whole picture. Jupiter goes all out, showering their mate with poetry, proclamations of love, and potential future scenarios, never mind the fact that the object of affection isn't ready for a serious relationship. Judgment may be an issue for those with shared Jupiter karma, making pie-in-the-sky promises or indulging another person's bad behavior or habits. Two people who exchange Jupiter karmic energy can discover their relationship resembles a hot air balloon ride—it feels really good going up, but no one ever planned on coming back down.

This placement can be quixotic, always tilting at windmills, like the quintessential God Jupiter himself, chasing wine, women, and good times. Yet in the fifth house, all good things must come to an end. We may wake up one morning to discover we've been sold an ice chest in Alaska, and may feel lied to—but we need to realize that our judgment about them was clouded, and that was *our* judgment. We can be delighted by their benevolence, feel lucky and blessed around them, but be wary of placing too much faith in one person. After all, every fifth house planet's missive is to equitably and honorably finish old business. Even if the relationship brought us nothing but happiness, Jupiter's no different.

Of all planets, judicious Jupiter can be philosophical about mistakes made, lessons learned, and grow from them. Jupiter in the fifth house knows how to seize opportunities that set its heart alight, realizing that holding back out of fear is pointless. Jupiter knows life is full of growth opportunities, trusting that no matter what happens, we always end up exactly where we need to be.

In summary, mates with whom you need to finish business may:
-Have a laissez faire or devil-may-care attitude.
-Carry the damning signature of moral authority, the King.
-Make promises that sound too good to be true.

If you have Jupiter in the fifth house: Whoever said that the best revenge is living well captured the karmic spirit of Jupiter medicine. For one person, that may mean living in a nice house on the hill; for another, taking regular spiritual retreats is expansive and faith-renewing. Each person's *dharma* (right path) is different, but whatever you do, it will feel gloriously renewing.

If you are in a relationship with a fifth house Jupiter: Hop onto their magic carpet, one where everything's possible—and you are in for a wild ride! Reach for the stars, together, but make sure at least one of you keeps your feet on terra firma, solid ground.

Your required romantic chemistry for a mate:
-Is generous, positive and uplifting to be around.
-Opens you to possibilities and new opportunities.
-Encourages you and believes in you.

Your playmates and creative catalysts are: Scholars, sages, gypsies, philosophers, teachers, priests, gurus, professors.

To renew the spark of passion: To live well is an affirmation of life. Introduce your partner to new experiences with different people and places that inspire possibility and meaning. A spiritual voyage or fantastic journey built for two? Yes! And keep the champagne flowing!

Fifth house Jupiter notables: Dalai Lama XIV, Arnold Schwarzenegger, Steven Spielberg, Janis Joplin, Frank Sinatra, Cary Grant, Bob Dylan, Jon Bon Jovi, Edgar Cayce, Marie Antoinette, Matthew McConaughey, Robin Williams, Hugh Hefner, Oscar Wilde, Ramana Maharishi, Amelia Earhart.

Saturn in the Fifth, or Capricorn on the Cusp: The Committed One

There are those who have a good idea, and at age eighty will still be talking about doing that idea. Then there are people who will locate that combination of fire and discipline within, and diligently commit their thoughts to book, film, or craft. They will finish that screenplay, career, or inventive idea, and at the end of life they will die satisfied that they sacrificed nights out, dates, and socializing for their creative baby. That's the type of person you'd expect to see with Saturn in the fifth house.

Sound easy? It's not. This isn't all gravy to fifth house Saturn, either. The kind of creative work they are here to perform requires slow, steady expenditures of effort over time, and a hefty degree of facing their own fears of failure and success. A law degree takes years to acquire, and a body of artistic work doesn't happen overnight. Sometimes their fear stops them in their tracks. However, they are built for manifesting something creative and tangible. This takes devotion. Whereas in the past, Saturn didn't have that chance to "selfishly" put in long hours in the recording studio, working on a craft or art they love; now they do, and they're ready to go the distance. Dedication is this person's strong suit.

The same goes for romance. Their romantic attitude may be cautious, slow and steady, not prematurely rushed; but once he or she is certain, fifth house Saturn is not afraid of saying "I do" and meaning it. Those born with Saturn in the fifth house know the power of a vow. When they give their heart, they mean it. And a partner who supports their creative solitude—all those hours spent at the office, library, or studio—is the one they love for life.

Your karmic mate is... devoted, committed, may make it difficult to get out of a vow, or want you to shoulder an unfair burden.

No one enters a relationship with a clean slate. When we partner up, we take on our mate's past baggage, debts, and burdens, and they take on ours. Children from a prior partnership can be a burden to the childless spouse. Our partner may have come with financial debts. During the relationship, one of us may get sick and become unable to work; the other may put in far longer hours at the office than we'd prefer. A natural part of every loving committed relationship includes shouldering these types of sacrifices without resentment, guilt, or blame.

Yet Saturn is the king of blame and guilt trips. Melissa Etheridge, who has a fifth house Saturn (in Aquarius), had a messy divorce with Tammy Lynn Michaels in 2010. Tammy accused Melissa of many things: loving her guitar more than Tammy or their kids, spending all her time in the studio rather than with the family, and asking Tammy to leave her job, claiming it left them broke and penniless. This is what dark shared Saturn karma looks like—demanding reparations from another person for burdens suffered, be they imagined or real.

The Saturn person has an ability (and perhaps a karmic duty) to keep his or her word in love relationships, and that's where things get complicated. On the positive side, this honorable intent fosters relationships built on promises made and vows kept, durability and resilience—strengths in any happy long-term partnership. But there's a warning here about keeping promises too long, long after the repayment period has ended. For the house of romance, fun, joy, and love freely given, there's nothing that takes the romance and joy out of love like the heavy stone of staying together out of duty or obligation to the partner, instead of love.

Loving another is not about shouldering burdens—it's about love. And yet people who share Saturn karma have a complicated history involving the repayment of debts and responsibilities. A lifetime ago, maybe they saved your behind and now it's time for you to save theirs. It's tricky, though, because while it's honorable to do the right thing, the right thing is never about sustained self-sacrifice and self-denial or begrudgingly giving in to another's prickly guilt demands. "The right thing" must always have heart and the Saturn person, for whom keeping a vow equals personal integrity, must be able to recognize when love and passion has left the relationship. In which case, cords should be cleanly cut.

This placement necessitates the fulfillment of a dutiful and honorable commitment to others for a period of time, and only so long as the action holds heart and dignity. If the contract loses touch with the excitement that brought two people together, if the relationship itself becomes a beast of burden and we continue in it out of a misguided sense of moral rightness or duty, the commitment creates future karma. And that's no fun at all.

In summary, mates with whom you need to finish business may:
-Appear to be emotionally inhibited, cold, stern.
-Be attached to making you feel guilty for a wrongdoing.
-Want to hold you accountable for not fulfilling a perceived obligation.

If you have Saturn in the fifth house: Work hard at something you love. This transcends teenage admiration and appreciation; a body of work you can be proud of commands the self-respect and integrity *you're* craving.

If you are in a relationship with a fifth house Saturn: Your mate is steadfast, true, and often too good at trading short-term pleasures for long-term rewards. Encourage them to relax and enjoy life, but respect their need for creative solitude too. Chances are, one of you has the tendency to lay burdens on the other—who accepts those all too readily. Don't do that!

Your required romantic chemistry for a mate:
-Maturity, pragmatism, a dry or understated sense of humor.
-Wears an air of authority, integrity and self-possession.
-Reliability. They do what they say and say what they mean.

Your playmates and creative catalysts are: Role models, wise elders, authorities, strategists, planners, professionals, comedians.

To renew the spark of passion: Maturity and humor are two qualities that renew your romantic partnership. Share a good belly laugh. Share coffee while balancing the bills and planning vacations. And every once in a while, have a conversation about how you're both feeling.

Fifth house Saturn notables: Bill Gates, Wolfgang Amadeus Mozart, Jim Morrison, Andy Warhol, Leonard Cohen, Raquel Welch, Katharine Hepburn, Deepak Chopra, Stevie Nicks, Maria Montessori, Melissa Etheridge.

Uranus in the Fifth, or Aquarius on the Cusp: The Individualist

How far would you go to risk being your self? Would you risk rejection from those you love, or heartbreak? From what we wear to work today (so that we won't get fired from our job), to what version of the story about our weekend we tell our boss versus our best friend, we make split-second decisions every day to present a socially acceptable version of ourselves to the people on whom we depend. We may tell our boss what he wants to hear so we can keep our job, but if we hide what we consider awkward or weird about ourselves from lovers and partners, we prevent ourselves from being fully seen and loved. These are the dilemmas a Uranian person faces.

The spiritual intent of people born with Uranus in the fifth house: To simply be themselves. If you're wondering how we can be anyone but ourselves, you're on the right track! Those born with Uranus have sacrificed their individuality and authenticity for acceptance and love in their karmic past, and this has hurt them. Cast in a script that didn't resemble who they were, now they yell the battle cry of the true self—*I gotta be me!* In the fifth house arenas of spontaneous play, creativity and romance, they need to break with social expectations, to embrace and express the naturally weird, different and iconoclastic sides of themselves. Whether on a date or in a creative partnership, they need to be upfront that they are a closet astrologer or are making a lifelong study of rare paint pigments. For Uranus, the weirder, the better. Authentic self-expression means holding nothing back.

Fifth house Uranus wears the mark of the individualist. Those with Uranus here have a pressing need to more naturally inhabit their original, spontaneous, and zany selves, which always involves being different from the mainstream. From presenting an authentic creative style to the world, to choosing individualistic, quirky, and bohemian lovers instead of status quo romances that lock us into deadening roles, the pressure of belonging to another may be strong—but the urge to be *me* is stronger.

Your karmic mate is... sexually exciting, different, unpredictable, may be unreliable, afraid of commitment, emotionally dissociated.

With Uranus in the vitalizing, creative, romantic fifth house, love is electrifying. The shared karma involves contracts with people who seem destined to wake us up in some creatively or sexually vitalizing way. If we have Uranus here, and social pressure has caused us to hide our sexual attraction for a different kind of lover or an unusual partnership, a Uranian mate will initiate us into the first real sexually satisfying encounter where we're fully seen and appreciated by another. They may free us up from ideas and conventions about how sex and love affairs "should" be. They may wake up our creativity. Conversely, we may have that effect on them, and on others—we can be a force of awakening for the world.

Uranus in the fifth says, "*Expect your sexual and creative urges to shock people.*" Latino star Ricky Martin has Uranus (Libra) here. Ricky came out as a gay man in a very macho culture. Frida Kahlo's, Uranus in the fifth house (Capricorn), open marriage and volatile romances with both sexes shocked everyone many decades ago, and her sexual openness is still considered progressive even by today's standards. People found the way Elvis Presley (Uranus in Aries in the fifth house) moved his body while performing, scandalous. These are the artists and lovers who push the envelope, people who make a statement with their unique sexual and creative self-expression.

Since romantic energy is linked to a need for sexual and romantic freedom, Uranus-born often find themselves unexpectedly magnetized by someone sexually exciting, who arouses that part of themselves that longs to be authentically (sometimes sexually or creatively) liberated. The chemistry of romance holds an electrifying charge of self-discovery for Uranus, though sometimes it seems that the only reason that this person appeared into their life was to wake them up. Sexual attractions come on suddenly, turning the Uranus person onto a path of awakening, but when the partnership has fulfilled its awakening role, it often fades just as quickly.

Those who share Uranian karma are guaranteed to raise a few eyebrows together—but be wary of a partner who is more committed to his or her autonomy than to you. Uranus finds it easy to get into exciting, but temporary, affairs with people who may be an extension of they want to do: live fearlessly, truly, and on their own terms.

The instant thrill of sexual consummation is exciting for a fifth house Uranus person, so when strong sexual lightning bolts strike hot, these two people can get into a lot of sexy trouble together. Although fun and exciting, the sex can be premature and have consequences—unintended pregnancy being one such biological consequence. As such, the decision to have children shouldn't be made lightly. Uranus needs to guard their freedom: parenthood can be another social expectation that limits them from pursuing their own authentic path. For the planet and person who is prompted to make up and then live by their own rules, there's not just one path to creative and sexual fulfillment—there are as many ways to live and love as there are stars in the sky.

In summary, mates with whom you need to finish business may:
-Be emotionally detached, unavailable, or unable to commit.
-Care about their freedom more than you.
-Be an eccentric individual on an entirely different path from you.

If you have Uranus in the fifth house: Cultivate a creative, artistic, or sexual identity that is 100%

unconcerned about what other people think of you. A creative outlet for imaginatively expressing what you *damn well please* is healing for you, and your authenticity inspires creative ventures.

Your required romantic chemistry for a mate:
-Is offbeat, different from the "type" your normally date or socialize with.
-They are an outsider, misfit and independent thinker.
-Has a radical, freedom-loving nature.

Your playmates and creative catalysts are: Awakeners, truth-tellers, rebels, geniuses, revolutionaries, individualists, exiles.

If you are in a relationship with a fifth house Uranus: Appreciate how different, quirky, and far from the mainstream they are, and prepare to be shocked by their unpredictability! Freedom and truth-to-self authenticity is essential for your relationship, but so is honoring the other's reality. Strive to give each other liberty, while not taking liberties with trust and respect.

To bring on the romance, or keep the spark of passion alive, you need: Put all your crazy cards on the table to spark a romantic connection, because everything that makes you different attracts others to you. Since predictability, routines, repetition, ennui, and boredom suck the life right out of a Uranian romance, cultivate a moving carousel of eccentric people, interests, and art to keep your romance stimulated, engaged, and alive.

Fifth house Uranus notables: Ricky Martin, Frida Kahlo, Drew Barrymore, Bob Dylan, Kate Hudson, Charlie Sheen, Juliette Lewis, Virginia Woolf, Martina Navratilova, Josephine Baker, Jack Osbourne, Zelda Fitzgerald, Howard Sasportas.

Neptune in the Fifth, or Pisces on the Cusp: The Enchanter/Enchantress

Everyday we face illusions of separation from loved ones, fear, physical sickness, and material poverty. We live in a universe that helps us to spiritually grow through duality, which leads many to believe this is our true experience (score one for illusion, zero for joy and truth). Yet Neptune, planet of divine compassion, bliss, and *all that is*, wants to reverse that trend. Those born with Neptune in the fifth house can see behind this dark curtain we call reality. They inform us that we are believing in the wrong things; why focus on material life when we could find meditative bliss in a spot of sunshine, a dance session, or our favorite love poem? Neptune invites us to play, laugh, live, and love from an expanded perspective.

Fifth house Neptune people can lasso angels in mid-flight, bringing heaven back to earth. They can do this through creating their own music, creativity, acting, channeling their fantasy life into art—art-making allows a direct portal through which spirit spontaneously flows. The soul intention of the fifth house Neptune person is to connect with divine consciousness and use that as fuel for creativity and self-expression. And have fun with it!

Spirituality isn't meant to be a painful drag, or deny and shame our bodily hungers. Prior life spiritual pursuits were likely overly disciplined, lacking Dionysian ecstasy, release, reverie, and bliss. Now those ties can be loosened and dissolved, and for the person with bacchanalian Neptune in the hedonistic fifth house, pleasures of spirit—and flesh—are to be pursued, both enthusiastically and reverentially. Neptune's openness to merging with others ensures ecstatic encounters with people who will take us deeper into that great mystery, love... as well as its inevitable impossibilities and losses. Loving and losing is not punishment, but part of becoming a bigger, more empathic being and ultimately, those with Neptune in the fifth, know this. Throughout the agony and the ecstasy, Neptune sings: "Your love lifted me higher than I've ever been lifted before."

Your karmic mate is... enchanting, spiritual, fantastic, and may be unreliable, unavailable, or mismatched as a long-term partner.

The fifth house Neptune person is one part magician, one part fantasy lover, and one part poet. Neptune approaches romantic love and falling in love similarly. They may find it easy to give themselves over to a lover, to surrender and ask for the same. They are sensitive (though not necessarily psychic), and can pick up a host of intuitive information from an initial encounter. Even meeting a potential lover can give rise to an instant understanding—which may or may not be rooted in karmic history—that we know each other from a prior life. Though that information may or may not be reliable.

Karmic contracts will trigger an existential longing to be released from the bondage of being human and to deeply merge with another in flesh and spirit. When two people sexually connect, it can feel like a deeply spiritual experience for the person born with Neptune in the fifth. A spontaneous romantic connection may feel immediately sacred and special. We may remember a past life together, or believe we've found The One.

Unfortunately, this says very little about whether a relationship has what it takes to go the distance. We all have hard edges and dissimilarities that will bump up against others, but initially in a courtship, Neptune won't look for these differences. Instead, Neptune seeks to dissolve all barriers, to merge with and join another. This planet's nature is formless, hazy, and dreamy.

Finding True Love is always a gamble, and with Neptune here, especially so. As Howard Sasportas says, "In the 5th, Neptune wins some and loses some." The process of discovering real, earthbound differences between us brings disillusionment to the Neptune relationship. We may have the red flags of our too-good-to-be-true romance; we may have misinterpreted another's motives and intentions; we may have dreamed up our lovers, casting them in a role they were ill-equipped to fulfill for us. Fifth house karma involves misuse of the love principle, and with this placement, no matter how spiritual, special, and kismet our love affair feels, we cannot make other people feel the same way towards us. We may only have their presence in our life for a time. On that note, our connection may indeed be timeless but not be *meant to be.* The danger of trying to turn a Neptune relationship into a long-term one is that two who are strong apart can grow weak together. And if they attempt to stay together, drama, chaos, and codependency ensues. This isn't a romantic portrait of "destined to be," but two lovers who refuse to face reality.

Neptune requires us to surrender our personal ego, including who and what our heart believes it most wants, for the deeper spiritual truths underlying our human existence. Heartbreak and loss can prove to be a spiritualizing experience for this placement, helping this person to form a deeper connection to the Divine Love in and around us—a source of love independent of conditions, or having another person available to love us back. If we don't find the spiritual maturity to turn to a bigger source for the love we need, we may continually project this need onto another, expecting our love interest to be our love supplier or the redeemer who makes our life worth living. Before true love can take root in our life, we can work on getting those needs met from Spirit instead of a mere mortal, someone who is only human, bound to disappoint and disillusion.

Neptune's longing for spiritual love, yearning for redemption through the eyes of the lover, and subsequent loss, suffering and disillusionment are experienced as deeply felt and personal—but they are simply experiences, no more our identity than passing clouds through a blue sky. Neptune teaches that love is not personal, but transcendent. Courtship may initially involve a heavy amount of projection, but by staying connected with a greater source, we can learn to see through the distortions and projections we carry. Then we're free to experience the ever-present flow of unconditional love running between, among, and within us.

In summary, mates with whom you need to finish business may:
-Evoke a special sense of destiny or fate about your connection.
-Not be upfront about their motives with you, are lost, unclear in themselves.

-Be escapist, chaotic, codependent, or out of touch with reality.

If you have Neptune in the fifth house: Dionysus (the Greek Neptune) had a mission to end care and worry through music, song, and poetry. You don't need to make this your mission. Just bring the magical, mysterious, timeless, and otherworldly dimensions into your life. Are you having fun yet? Spiritual pursuits that involve exploring alternate dimensions of perception and direct consciousness should be always be pleasurable for you

If you are in a relationship with a fifth house Neptune: You're in for a treat—tender, sensitive, goo-goo-eyed Neptune takes romance to the next level! Since one, or both of you may be unrealistic about what this relationship can do for either of you, keep your attachments and expectations for each other light.

Your required romantic chemistry for a mate:
-Is compassionate, gentle and sensitive.
-Has a spiritual or mystical nature that intrigues you.
-Is creative, imaginative, and soulful.

Your playmates and creative catalysts are: Poets, dreamers, visionaries, mystics, artists, spiritual teachers.

To renew the spark of passion: Life has its share of noises and distractions. To renew your spark, create an environment or activity where you can be quietly transported together. Share moments of silent, timeless tenderness reading poetry, eye-gaze over candlelight, explore tantra, and spend time in nature. Spirituality has a place for you two, though it shouldn't be laden with dogma, but grounded in shared pleasures.

Fifth house Neptune notables: Carla Bruni Sarkozy, Celine Dion, Paulo Coelho, Karen Carpenter, Cindy Crawford, Mick Jagger, Che Guevara, Charles Manson, Marianne Williamson, Carlos Santana, Robert (Bobby) Kennedy, Brian Wilson, Richard Tarnas, F. Scott Fitzgerald, Carl Sagan, Angelina Jolie, Martin Luther King Jr.

Pluto in the Fifth House, or Scorpio on the Cusp: The Sorcerer/Sorceress

Imagine seeing sexual violence on television for the first time as a child, when you don't yet have the maturity or psychological sophistication to handle this complex information. Where do the feelings go? Deep down. As children, we face a wide range of dark knowledge and 99% of us have little recourse but to repress the strong feelings that accompany witnessing abuse and violence.

Those born with Pluto in the fifth house were exposed to the dark shadows of humanity early in life, and consequently it's taken a toll on their ability to meet life with trust. Their childlike innocence, spontaneity, joy, and ability to jump into life and love with trust that *we will be okay* has been Plutonified. If we have Pluto here, we believe that, on some level, *life is not safe or okay*, and *people hurt each other*, because we've witnessed that. This awareness rocks our world and darkens our fifth house playground, our place of confidence, elan. As in a Brothers Grimm fairytale, where every innocent has a counterpart waiting in the dark forest with a poison apple, we become suspicious—often rightly so.

Old tapes can distort our lives. If our ability to feel safe in the world has been compromised, to heal, our natural confidence has been wounded. To restore that, the fifth house Pluto person must learn to spontaneously allow old blocked, backlogged emotions and pain to hiccup and flow. We've got to feel it to heal it—but do so without becoming so self-identified with the cathartic process that we get stuck there. Pluto's presence generates both intense ego focus and creative strength. Instead of being a problem, intense feelings of betrayal, loss, pain, and grief need to be accepted as part of their natural process. A creative outlet helps immensely, and so do playmates!

A natural playmate is a romp in the hay with teeth. Honest, psychologically sophisticated, and courageously openhearted, they have an ability to "go there"—go to places inside which might scare a lesser human. These souls will cheerlead fifth house Pluto people with humor and perspective, helping them to be a force in their own right, encouraging their talents and fostering trust. That's when they know it's safe to come out and play.

Your karmic mate is... sexually exciting, psychologically insightful, and won't reveal his or her deep self or wounds and secrets to you.

Imagine the common phenomenon of having sex with someone before you both fall in love. Date one: You experience instant chemistry and soulfulness. Date two: You can't keep your hands off each other, and you have sex. Date three: They avoid your phone calls. You psychoanalyze them with your friends and fret over their lack of responsiveness. Next, feelings of abandonment and hurt probably arise, as you also realize you cared more than you claimed. Or maybe the situation is reverse; you are on the receiving end of their sharing. You thought it was casual sex, but now you want to flee.

What happened? Sex is sporty and fun in the fifth house, but Pluto is no lightweight planet! If we have Pluto in the fifth house of casual dating, we may underestimate our ability to have a casual sexual relationship, as Pluto's nature is to bare it all and "go all the way". Pluto holds our deepest secrets, unconscious wounds, and trapdoors, and so even as we're having fun, the intensity of our unconscious material builds and seeks expression. After a relatively brief time together, things get *real*. How does this Pluto stimulation play out in our practical life? Our sensitivities are plucked in a simple disagreement, or a piece of information casually revealed doesn't feel casual to us. One unreturned phone call brings up memories of being betrayed or abandoned. If we look deep enough, we may realize that underneath our emotional reaction, we are so deeply afraid of being hurt all over again.

We may realize that those initial steps of courtship, which seem so easy for everyone else to navigate, deeply undo us. To work with this, it helps to sexually slow down. The fifth house generates impulsivity and sexual excitement, but Pluto needs time to assess a partner's affinities and incompatibilities, intentions and motives, and his or her own as well. Pluto karma involves meeting our deepest wounds through people we may know very little about—even as we think they know us.

With Pluto here, be alert to how soon and how much material both you and the other share. Fifth house Pluto can compulsively share too much too soon without waiting to see if the other is being open and truthful, or is available for a relationship. As much as Pluto is inclined to "go all the way" on the first date, there's a natural progression to intimacy we need to *allow* to happen. With Pluto in the house of courtship, your courtship ritual may mean facing the madness and the craziness in yourself and your partner—before you jump into bed.

The fifth house Pluto person carries the Plutonian signature of erotic magnetism and energetic intensity, effectively drawing in the right partners who will help him or her do the deeper work of soul healing. Ideally, shared relationship karma doesn't damage us. It lances the original wound, inviting us to go beyond the sting of being jilted, betrayed, or abandoned, so that we finally ask ourselves: *When was the very first time I felt this way?* Then we take that information in and self-heal.

Pluto can be obsessive. Beware of any compulsion you have to buy a one-way ticket to a lifelong relationship. Instead, learn to hold a compassionate space for honest and self-aware conversation and soul-sharing, without attaching yourself to them like an appendage, or needing to know where the relationship is headed. Do this, and you arrive at the fifth house promise: fun.

In summary, mates with whom you need to finish business may:

-Be secretive, manipulative, emotionally closed, or defensive; are wounded themselves.

-Give advice but be unwilling to share their deep selves and history with you.

-Strongly respond to your sexual magnetism, but don't want/are unavailable for a commitment.

If you have Pluto in the fifth house: Accept all of your spontaneous processes and inner workings as good and natural. Explore and investigate them without getting too hung up on them or making your wounds "special". We all have a Pluto! Tears, laughter, grieving, and forgiveness help you to enjoy life and have fun again.

If you are in a relationship with a fifth house Pluto: Intense, psychologically perceptive, and sexually magnetic—that's no vampire, that's your lover! Enjoy the sexy chemistry. Chances are, one or both of you are either too dramatic or secretive about your feelings. Be real with each other then give it space to chill.

Your required romantic chemistry for a mate:
-Perceptiveness, insightfulness, penetrating eye contact.
-An aura of mystery, smoldering sexual magnetism, power.
--They are frank, truthful, but know when it's more appropriate to not be an open book.

Your playmates and creative catalysts are: Psychologists, shamans, therapists, detectives, sorcerers, researchers.

To renew the spark of passion you need: Intensity, creativity, and gritty psychological honesty gets you going. Bring your warm-blooded sexuality to pursuits of pleasure; share and bare it all! Creative interests and hobbies hold hours of shared joy and pleasure for you.

Fifth house Pluto notables: Johnny Cash, Sheryl Crow, John Lennon, Robert Redford, Halle Berry, Audrey Hepburn, Drew Barrymore, Charlie Sheen, Tony Blair, Coco Chanel, Carlos Castaneda, Stevie Nicks, Sylvia Plath, Hunter Thompson, Billie Holiday, William Blake.

My Favorite Mistake

Astrologer Steven Forrest has called a fifth house love affair "my favorite mistake." Sheryl Crow wrote song by the same title about a doomed, passionate love for an unfaithful lover who, for all the heartbreak caused, remains her favorite mistake. There was speculation about the song's subject (was it Jakob Dylan? Eric Clapton?), but with privacy-loving Pluto in Sheryl's fifth house, we may never know the true subject of her passion. One of her dearest relationships was with Owen Wilson, a Sun in Scorpio born (Pluto's zodiac sign), who was reportedly unfaithful to her. Incidentally, Sheryl named her child, Owen, after him (the fifth house rules children). Owen attempted suicide (Pluto is also the planet ruling death) that same year. The character of our fifth house mates may or may not be Plutonian, but we all know what it's like to be hooked on someone's energy even as we know they are unhealthy or wrong for us. If you have a fifth house planet, you probably have a favorite mistake, too!

South Node in the Fifth House: The Futurist

The South Node is not a planet, but an invisible point in the sky where the Moon's path crosses the ecliptic. As such, it does not describe your mate's character (refer to the sign on the fifth house cusp for this information). However, the Moon's nodal axis does have associations with karmic behaviors and tendencies that can cause us to have difficulty with others.

With the South Node here, it's easy for you to get pulled backward into unsatisfying attitudes and behaviors in love and pleasure seeking. You've spent prior lifetime(s) living in the present moment, developing your capacity for entertaining, recreational activities, and enjoying life to the fullest. You may have also racked up a lot of experience with short-term romantic partners. While these behaviors are not inherently wrong in and of themselves, you may have overdeveloped this tendency at the cost of other areas of your life. Time spent focused on the present moment can cause us to lose sight of our goals, and so can focusing exclusively on a love affair to the downfall of our kingdom. Shortsightedness, favoring the thrill of the moment, can cause us to lack forward vision. The shadow of your South Node zodiac sign also points to specific behaviors that lead to dissipation.

To counteract this backward pulling tendency of the South Node, look beyond the present. Think strategically about the future. Make plans and goals, then enlist support. Ask yourself: Am I spinning my wheels in a relationship? Am I partnering and dating people for brief periods who are, at best, a gamble? Try to regard all your relationships as you would an investment, always being alert to whether they are leaking energy from your life or returning energy dividends. When dating, make the affirmative answer to the question, "Do we have a future together?" paramount.

Amanda Knox, the American teenager who was held in Italian prison for three years after being accused of killing her roommate, has South Node (in Libra) in the fifth house. Known as a "party girl" for her immaturity, love for recreational fun, and drinking, these behaviors played an unfortunate role in how she was portrayed by prosecutors at her murder trial.

North Node in the Fifth House: The Playmate

The North Node is not a planet, but an invisible point in the sky where the Moon's path crosses the ecliptic. As such, it does not describe your mate's character (refer to the sign on the fifth house cusp for this information). However, the Moon's nodal axis does have associations with karmic behaviors and tendencies that can cause us to have difficulty with others.

The North Node here alerts us to an area of life with which we are least acquainted, and therefore holds great potential for great growth. The good news is the astrological gods want you to have far more fun, love affairs, and recreation. You've spent far too much time in prior lifetime(s) living in the future, creating a strategy, trying to anticipate any unseen angles. You've compulsively planned, steered, and held committee meetings about a future that may or may not happen. As such, your all-too-easy habit of premeditated planning has taken you away from living in the spontaneous present moment. Somewhere along the way, you may have lost touch with the childlike abandon and trust you need to play, have fun, and fall in love.

There are helpful attitudes you can cultivate in yourself, like spontaneity, romance, a sense of adventure, and whimsy. A creative hobby, sport, or art form serves this aim well. Spending time with playmates who encourage spontaneity helps to loosen your need to be in control. Hang out with artists and creative types—they are often really good at living in the moment. Make it your goal to be the first person your friends think of when they discover they have an extra ticket to a rock concert or art exhibit. In other words, and in no uncertain terms, have fun. Learn to trust that the world won't fall apart while you're not looking. Your spiritual growth requires it! Look to the strengths of your North Node zodiac sign for helpful attitudes and behaviors to cultivate.

Romantic relationships, dating, and taking a chance on love may feel like a huge gamble, but don't be afraid to explore new and varied relationships. Take a cue from

Demi Moore, who has North Node (in Leo) in the fifth house. Demi is attached to being productive and planning life from all angles, but taking creative artistic risks and having a variety of romantic partners motivates her growth. Becoming a performer was a good move for Demi, as was her pairing with the much younger Ashton Kutcher.

Section 4

Learning to Love and Let Go

The answer is easy if you take it logically, I'd like to help you in your struggle to be free. There must be fifty ways to leave your lover. —Paul Simon and Art Garfunkel

Short-term relationships have the power to resolve longstanding karma, which is essentially soul-freeing. We've covered the qualities of a karmic partnership generally and astrologically. So how to know when and if a relationship has a future? It's a personal knowing, and one only your heart knows. But if we're pining for someone or something that's just not working—we're heartfelt, intentional, conscious, and we've put in the good effort and it's still not satisfying—maybe it's time to let go.

Diving into the question of how much work to put into a committed partnership before deciding to leave is beyond the scope of this book. Naturally, a marriage or any long-term partnership takes work. Since the nature of a fifth house relationship is temporary, we can simply say, *when love becomes more limiting and painful than joyful, it's time to move on.*

With karmic partners, there will come a time when staying with a person will bring us more suffering than joy, will limit our choices and ability to direct our own destiny, and potentially perpetuate psychological baggage for not just the two of us, but children or other mates. When love becomes more limiting and difficult than freeing and joyful, that's not love—that's emotional attachment, and this can create future suffering.

Breaking up can be a process, especially if we've built a life together—there are children, mortgages, and a history of deeply shared love. Leaving a loved one is usually not as complex as we make it out to be—it is emotionally difficult. In the Simon and Garfunkel song, a mistress sang to a pained husband trying to leave his wife: "the answer is easy if you take it logically," yet the heart isn't logical. Some endings are necessarily quick and, like pulling off a Band-Aid, momentarily sharp in their pain, while others are more emotionally dramatic and prolonged, like a long opera. There is no right way to leave, but if it is a fifth house relationship that has run its course, leave we must.

At any ending, our attitude and what we are able to glean from the relationship can make all the difference between parting in peace and understanding, or in animosity and embittered pain... and future karmic contracts to resolve. To truly end shared karma, we must do so honorably and with care. This includes treating the other person with dignity, kindness, and respect.

Should I Stay or Should I Go?

A friend stays with a partner who is disrespectful and abusive. Who among us hasn't played the role of the supportive friend while secretly palm-slapping our forehead? It's a human conflict. Sometimes one part of us is desperately unhappy in a relationship, while another part of us still derives satisfaction from it, and the net effect paralyzes us. If you are questioning whether you should love them or leave them, sit down with pen and paper and honestly answer the following questions, summarized from the book *Too Good to Leave, Too Bad to Stay* by Mira Kirshenbaum.

1. Are you getting your needs met in the partnership without too much effort?

2. Do you genuinely like your partner and does your partner like you?

3. Do you feel a spark of sexual attraction between you?

4. Does your partner demonstrate behavior that he or she is unwilling or unable to change?

5. Do you see yourself when you look in your partner's eyes?

6. Do you respect each other as individuals?

7. Do they serve as a resource for you in a way that enhances your life?

8. Do you have fun together?

9. Does your relationship have the demonstrated capacity for forgiveness?

10. Do you and your partner have mutual goals and dreams for your future together?

11. If God or a divine being gave you permission to leave, would you finally feel like it was okay to leave?

Seeing Things for the First Time

If you have a troubling relationship, imagine that this person is a placeholder for your growth, someone holding the space for you to learn how to do any number of things: stand up for yourself, express yourself, or even to forgive. Imagine they once agreed to help you evolve. This may be a big leap to ask, and for those who have been in emotionally or physically abusive relationships, this may be an uncomfortable thought. However, the work of past-life regressionists like Michael Newton and Roger Woolgers has demonstrated that such contracts do exist. What if the hurt you thought another inflicted was actually a lesson your soul chose to experience in order to learn and grow in capability? It's certainly a more empowering thought than feeling victimized by circumstances and people who seem to cause trouble for us. This perspective may challenge your beliefs. Yet if we believe in a benevolent and intelligent Universe, we may also consider that life is not random, but meaningful and elegantly organized. If we believe we are not victims of our fate, but have free will, we may also entertain the thought that we've always had free will—even the free will to choose our teacher-partners for this lifetime.

Forgiveness

What does it mean to truly forgive, and receive forgiveness from, another person? If we have religious roots in our culture, we may think forgiveness is earned, a pious pursuit involving self-flagellation, confession, and a dispensation of clemency or absolution from another. This may sound extreme to some ears, but these ancient beliefs still influence us. We may believe that until we have the opportunity to express hurt, parse out the various infractions, and apologize, we cannot forgive and move on. Whether writing a letter we'll never mail, going to the confessional, or having that one last chance to sit down and rehash what really went wrong, we tend to think that forgiveness has conditions. I'm not sure that's what the original meaning of forgiveness is about.

Forgiveness is being able to let go. It's simply letting go. That doesn't mean it's simple, nor does it mean that we forgive and forget. Most of us never forget—at least not the big infractions, and nor should we. Why would I want to forget that I've walked into the same old hurtful fire with another person five times past, and keep doing it again? To forgive, we find a way to get to the place in ourselves where that person no longer carries a charge. This can be done with others, or within ourselves.

There are many ways to work on letting go: rituals, affirmations, letter and journal writing, prayer, cathartically releasing anger, therapy. Emotional freedom technique (EFT) is one of my favorite ways to process difficult emotions and let them go. It matters less how you do it, but that you *do* it. Do what works for you. You will know that you've really let go of an old grudge or attachment when you are no longer triggered by an old resentment or wounding story—when the mention of their name or bumping into them at the grocery store no longer causes you to see red, send shooting pain through your heart, or send you running to your therapist.

Why do we need to bother with forgiveness, besides our peace of mind? Emotional attachment creates karma. We tend to think only events have karma, but our emotional responses also create karma. For instance, think of a national tragedy and how that affects people for decades, even generations, later. People carry the impact of such events in their hearts, sending ripples into their lives and those of others. The heart is that powerful.

Anything we're attached to—be it resentment, a yearning for a person to be who they are not, broken-heartedness—when we can finally say, "okay, it's no big deal," we have truly forgiven. That's the essence of what it means to forgive. Once, on one of my visits to Austria with my husband, we met an ex-Nazi officer from World War II who spent several years as a prisoner in an American prisoner-of-war camp. When he told this story to us Americans, we naturally became uncomfortable, until he said, "Don't worry... I forgave America long ago." This was a powerful moment. When thinking about the atrocities humans are capable of forgiving, the small stones I carry in my own heart seemed petty. We all live with injustices, and we are all capable of forgiveness.

It may take inner work, but there's incredible value in forgiving another. We can finish a painful contract and truly be free. Of course, we don't have to forgive. None of us do. But know that when we don't forgive someone, it's a choice—somewhere inside, we don't want to let go. Be honest with yourself here. By honestly acknowledging that a part of you *really doesn't want to let go*, the part of you that really *does* want to let go—the part of you that wants freedom for yourself and the other person—can take the next step toward forgiveness.

Affirmations for forgiveness and release (repeat as needed):

"I now release and am released from those who are no longer part of the divine plan of my life, as they now release me and find their good elsewhere. I expand quickly into the divine plan of my life where all conditions are permanently perfect."

"You are in my life by divine appointment. You have crossed my path so that I may learn something from you, and so that I may give you my blessing. I now do this and you are released to your highest good."

The Clarity of Hindsight

When one door closes, another opens; but we often look so long and so regretfully upon the closed door that we do not see the one which has opened for us. —Alexander Graham Bell

Attraction drives us to do strange things, including attaching ourselves like an appendage to people who, while good for us today, may not be good for us tomorrow. Today, we may think they hang the Moon and set the Sun, but little did we know our karmic mate was only meant to send fireworks surging through our soul for a time. Hindsight is always 50/50, right?

Few of us are so enlightened that we avoid errors in judgment; sometimes hindsight is all we have to go on. In the aftermath of things not working out, forced to wrestle the dragon of disappointment and a broken heart, all we can do is process the pain. But what if we also explored our connection from a higher perspective? What if we focused on the love essence of our exchange, instead of how they let us down? *What did they give us, and what did we give them? Were they a catalyst for us?*

How would the choices we made in our life be different today without having known them?

It's tempting to overlook a relationship's greater gifts and focus on how it ends up, especially if we were wronged or betrayed. We focus on all the grudges, disappointments, unmet desires, and resentments, and allow them to fester inside instead of seeing the blessings they bestowed. They came into our lives for a reason. If we dig around deep enough, we are sure to find a parting gift, if not several. Are we clear enough to see what they gave us?

Perhaps this gift can often only be bartered in hindsight, after we're set free of our attachment, after we've had time to grieve its loss. But whenever we're ready to turn a corner on that page, to look at our love from a different angle, we can ask ourselves several questions.

Ten Questions to Ask Yourself After It's Over

Think of any short-term relationship that still weighs heavy on your heart. Maybe they wronged you or broke your heart, and you haven't forgiven them. Maybe they hurt and betrayed you, or were "the one that got away." Maybe you viewed the relationship as a failure, or yourself as having failed them. Ask yourself these questions, writing down your first response.

1. Did they overtly or serendipitously influence a major life decision you might not have made without them? Like the choice to go back to school, start a business, move to another state, pick up a book, or take a trip? Did that choice influence another decision that changed your life?

2. Did this person serve as a catalyst, offering you his or her influential, dynamic, or disruptive energy so something else could happen?

3. Did they show you a talent, gift, or strength you wouldn't have acknowledged otherwise? Identify at least one gift they gave you.

4. If you felt you shouldered an unfair burden in the relationship, what personal strength did you develop as a result of carrying that burden?

5. Did your relationship attempt to help you resolve a conflict or heal an ancient wound you'd been carrying with you for a long time?

6. Can you think of one good reason to continue being bitter, angry, unforgiving, or resentful toward this person (trick question—the only good reason being, of course, your own happiness and peace)?

7. Did they help you see a part of yourself with which you were previously unfamiliar, felt ashamed of, or felt under-recognized or unloved for?

8. Did they introduce you to a friend or group of people who proved influential in your life?

9. Can you see that you always had power, free will, and choice in this situation with this person?

10. From a higher perspective, can you see the lesson this relationship taught you? Can you feel gratitude for this?

No Timeline for Grief

Real love stories never have endings. —Richard Bach

Separation from a significant loved one is like a death, and we each have our own timeline for grieving a loss. We can't rush letting go. Their weird idiosyncrasies, things we really liked about them—their smell, their smile, the way they made our eggs, the sound of their voice—can bring us to tears.

The heart is limitless in its ability to love. I once read that a year after his death, Patrick Swayze's widow Lisa Neimi was still texting "I love you" to her husband just before she got on an airplane, just as she did when he was alive. Bereavement rituals that seem odd to one person will heal another. Even keeping an ex's belongings around can be a healthy part of coping with loss. Our culture likes to rush letting go. We hurry up after the funeral or divorce to move the person's belongings and clothing quickly out of sight. Out of sight, out of mind, they say... but as any person who has lost a loved one knows, they are always on our mind. The heart knows no timeline.

A relationship's end doesn't mean it's over, not on the inside. An ending offers another type of beginning—to take up one's own inner journey. There's nothing like loss to help you see the sharp, honest landscape of your own life—how you've been procrastinating, in denial about things, that you aren't the person you imagined yourself as being, or living the life you have always wanted. Death and loss, and the feelings of desolation and regret it brings, can be the wake-up call to finally step into the emotional issues you've been avoiding so that you can more fully live. There are invaluable resources available for helping to cope and heal through loss, including friends, support groups, counselors, and books. Among my favorites, *When Things Fall Apart, The Places That Scare You,* and *The Wisdom of No Escape*, all by Buddhist author Pema Chodron, and *Broken Open: How Difficult Times Can Help Us Grow*, by Elizabeth Lesser.

Yet, it is important to move on from your fifth house mate. Love has many faces. Your karmic or time-of-life mate showed you one face. They activated something inside of you, they gave you a gift—passion, power, romance, a spark of life force—when you needed it. They showed you what you are capable of. Just because it wasn't meant to last forever doesn't make it any less precious. Even though it ends, the gifts of love remain.

All beings are here to help us learn and grow. If this feels negative to you or causes you suffering and grief, you don't have to carry your negative feelings, attitudes, or connection to this person forward into the future. You can finish this. You can love, you can learn... and you can let go.

Appendix

How to Locate the Fifth House in Your Chart

1. Obtain your birth chart. Head over to www.astro.com and enter your birth details (birth date, time, and place) to receive a free copy of your birth chart.

2. Your chart will look something like this. What is this beautiful madness? Looking upward, this is a snapshot of the heavens at the exact place and moment you were born.

3. There are 12 constellations organizing our sky and this is reflected in the 360-degree circle of your birth chart, divided into twelve sectors, or astrological houses. You may notice that house sizes vary. Some are big while others are small, due to the location in which you were born (the further north or south you were born from the equator, the more extreme the differences in house sizes will be). Each zodiac sign is always allotted 30 degrees (30x12=360 degrees of a circle), but some houses will contain more or less than that, with the degrees of one zodiac sign spilling into the next house or beginning mid-way at a house cusp. Beginners, take note: the size of your house of "love" or "money" is not a reflection of how much or how little you will have of either!

4. Locate your fifth house. To do this, first imagine the chart is a clock. At 9 o'clock is the easternmost point, the cusp of the first house, also called the Ascendant (or Rising). At 6 o'clock is the southernmost point of the chart, the cusp of the fourth house or the Imum Coeli. At 3 o'clock is the westernmost point of the chart, the cusp of the seventh house, also the Descendant. At high noon is the northernmost point, the cusp of the tenth house, the MidHeaven. The Ascendant (ASC), Imum Coeli (IC), Descendant (DSC), Midheaven (MC) are known as the

four angles of your birth chart. So where does your fifth
house begin? At 5 o'clock. Your sixth house begins at 4
o'clock, your seventh house at 3 o'clock, and so on.

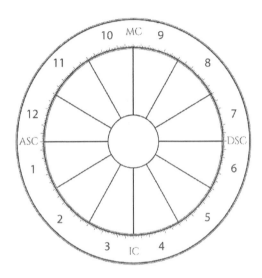

5. What is the sign on the cusp of your fifth house? Find
the symbols for each zodiac sign, Aries through Pisces,
located in the column below. Look to the sign at the
beginning, or on the cusp, of your fifth house (5 o'clock).
Your cusp sign shows your motivating behavior and
approach toward this area of life. For instance, if you
have Pisces on the fifth house cusp, your experience of
romance is colored by the imaginative, highly idealized,

intuitive and sometimes chaotic, fantasy-based sign of
Pisces (see: Planets and Signs in the Fifth House).

Sun	☉	♈	Aries
Moon	☽	♉	Taurus
Mercury	☿	♊	Gemini
Venus	♀	♋	Cancer
Mars	♂	♌	Leo
Jupiter	♃	♍	Virgo
Saturn	♄	♎	Libra
Uranus	♅	♏	Scorpio
Neptune	♆	♐	Sagittarius
Pluto	♇	♑	Capricorn
North Node	☊	♒	Aquarius
South Node	☋	♓	Pisces

6. Are there any planets in your fifth house? To find the planet in your fifth house, refer to the left hand of the column above. Planets indicate energy and action, so you will expend more energy in an area of life, or house, that has many planets (planets = action). No planets? That's okay. There are only 10 planets (including the Moon), so it is impossible to have planets in every house. Houses that don't have planets may be empty, but they are not lifeless. The goings-on of this house are mediated by the sign on the cusp of the house, that sign's ruling planet, and the moving planets transiting through that house (transits).

7. Do you want to know more? My favorite books for astrology beginners are *Astrology for Yourself* by Demetra George and Douglas Bloch, *The Inner Sky* by Steven Forrest, and my friend April Elliott Kent's book, *The Essential Guide to Practical Astrology*.

For Further Understanding

Forrest, Steven and Jodie. Skymates: Love, Sex and Evolutionary Astrology. Chapel Hill, NC: Seven Paws Press, 2002.

Gerhardt, Dana. *The Fifth House*. Article, retrieved from astro.com

Hickey, Isabel. Astrology: A Cosmic Science. Sebastopol, CA: CRCS Publications. 1992.

Sasportas, Howard. The Twelve Houses: Understanding the Importance of the Houses in your Astrological Birthchart. Hammersmith, London: Aquarian Press, 1998.

About the Author

Author of *A Love Alchemist's Notebook* and *Venus Signs*, Jessica Shepherd has studied astrology since 1992, and has been practicing and writing about astrology since 2003 at Moonkissd.com. She specializes in counseling people through transition, personal growth, and awakening. Jessica holds a bachelor's degree (B.A.) in art and business and is a certified health coach. Her health coaching website is: http://www.jessicashepherd.net.

Jessica loves fan mail!

You can write to Jessica at:

moonkissd@moonkissd.com

Acknowledgements

Many thanks to my friends and clients—my guinea pigs—for helping me to understand how fifth house planets actually work in real life. I am so deeply indebted to the astrologers who have studied this topic before me. We are all standing on the shoulders of others, and I am standing on Steven Forrest's, Isabel Hickey's, Howard Sasportas', Liz Greene's shoulders... to name just a few.

Thank you to Astrodatabank.com, from which the celebrity names for "fifth house notables" were compiled.

Deep gratitude also goes out to the editors of this book, Ania Szremski and Isabelle Anne Abraham, and the designer of this cover, Nada Orlic. And to John, my husband, who always knows just how to help when I get stuck. To Erin Reese, for her initial help in editing and naming this book. Thank you to Terri Jensen, client and friend, for generously sharing her fifth house experience. Finally, I thank you, dear reader, for supporting my work. Without you, I would still be writing in my journal instead sharing these thoughts with the world.

-Jessica

More from Jessica Shepherd

Available at: http://www.moonkissd.com.

BOOKS

Venus Signs: Discover Your Erotic Gifts & Secret
Desires Through Astrology (Llewellyn, 2015)

A Love Alchemist's Notebook: Magical Secrets For
Drawing Your True Love Into Your Life (Llewellyn,
2010)

35038914R00092

Made in the USA
Middletown, DE
16 September 2016